NORWAY TOUR GUIDE:

Unveiling Norway, a Journey Through Nordic Enchantment With First Timers Tips And A Basic Itinerary

Tamara Horan

I remember the day I set foot in Norway, eager to start on a journey that would unravel the country's enchanting beauty. From the moment I arrived in Oslo, I could feel the allure of this Nordic wonderland. The vibrant city received me with open arms, and I knew that my adventure was about to begin.

Wandering through the streets of Oslo, I marveled at the juxtaposition of technology and history. The sleek design of the Opera House stood in stark contrast to the medieval charm of the Akershus Fortress. As I explored the city's cultural treasures, such as the National Gallery and its impressive collection of Norwegian art, I felt a deep connection with the country's rich history.

Leaving the bustling city behind, I went into the breathtaking landscapes of Norway. The fjords, with their majestic cliffs and shimmering seas, held a magnetic pull. I went on a boat tour through the world-renowned Geirangerfjord, marveling at the sheer grandeur of nature. The cascading waterfalls and verdant valleys left me in awe, and I couldn't help but feel a profound sense of tranquility amidst such natural beauty.

The trip continued as I made my way to the charming city of Bergen. Surrounded by seven mountains, this picturesque destination gave a perfect blend of culture and nature. Exploring the historic Bryggen Wharf, a UNESCO World Heritage site, I dove into the city's Hanseatic past. The colorful wooden buildings and cobblestone streets exuded a timeless charm that took me back in time.

Immersing myself in the local food was a delightful adventure in itself. From savoring newly caught seafood in coastal villages to indulging in traditional Norwegian delicacies like lutefisk and reindeer meat, my taste buds were constantly tantalized. I also found the joy of exploring local markets, where

I tasted an array of artisanal cheeses, cured meats, and freshly baked pastries.

As the nights grew longer, I found myself in the magical world of the Northern Lights. In the remote areas of Tromso, I chased the ethereal dance of colors across the Arctic sky. The sheer magnificence of this natural occurrence left me spellbound, as if I had stepped into a fairytale.

Throughout my journey, I experienced the warmth and hospitality of the Norwegian people. Whether it was sharing stories with locals in a cozy café or joining in traditional folk dances during a summer event, I felt a sense of belonging in this land of fjords and folklore.

Now, as I sit down to pen this trip guidebook, I am filled with a sense of purpose. I want to share the wonders of Norway, to make the road easier for fellow travelers seeking their own adventures.

Through these pages, I hope to capture the essence of this captivating country and inspire others to start on their own unforgettable journey through the land of the midnight sun and the land of the Northern Lights.

Introduction to Norway

1.1 Overview of the Nation

Norway is a Nordic nation in Northern Europe, officially known as the Kingdom of Norway. It has lengthy coastlines along the North Atlantic Ocean and the Barents Sea to the west and north, as well as shared borders with Sweden to the east, Finland to the northeast, and Russia to the northwest. Here is a summary of some significant features of Norway:

Geographical Features: With its spectacular fjords, untamed mountains, enormous forests, and clear lakes, Norway is known for its breathtaking natural beauty. The nation is well-known for its varied topography, which includes the well-known fjords of western Norway including the Geirangerfjord and the Naeryfjord, which are listed as UNESCO World Heritage Sites.

Oslo, which is in the southern half of the country, is the capital city of Norway. Other prominent cities are Trondheim, Troms, Bergen, Stavanger, and Stavanger. Each city offers a variety of cultural, historical, and outdoor events in addition to having its own distinct charm.

Norway is a constitutional monarchy with a parliamentary democratic style of government. The head of government is the Prime Minister, whereas the ceremonial head of state is the King of Norway, presently King Harald V. The social assistance system, progressive laws, and high standard of living in Norway are well-known.

Norway's economy is thriving and well-developed. It is also known for having a plethora of natural resources, especially oil and gas deposits, which have greatly boosted the nation's prosperity. One of the biggest sovereign wealth funds in the world, the Government Pension Fund Global, is responsible for managing Norway's petroleum resources. In addition to oil and gas, the Norwegian economy also relies heavily on technology, fisheries, tourism, maritime industries, and renewable energy.

Norwegian culture and heritage are rich in customs, folklore, and Viking ancestry. The nation is proud of its literary heritage, which includes works by well-known writers like Henrik Ibsen and Knut Hamsun. The beloved cultural traditions of Norway include "folkemusikk," a term for traditional music, and "bunad," a term for traditional clothing. Skiing and biathlon are two other winter sports that are well-known in Norway.

Education and innovation are very important in Norway, which is also renowned for its top-notch educational institutions. Many institutions and colleges in the nation provide a variety of academic programs, including English-taught courses for visitors. Furthermore, Norway is a leader in innovation, particularly in the areas of technology, environmental sustainability, and renewable energy.
Norway has a wide range of chances for outdoor enthusiasts interested in nature and outdoor activities. There are numerous outdoor activities available, including hiking and camping in national parks like Jotunheimen and Rondane, as well as fishing, skiing, and snowboarding in the winter. Visitors are drawn to the northern regions of Norway by the Aurora Borealis, a natural phenomenon.

1.2 Brief History

Earlier times:
The history of Norway extends back to the Paleolithic Age. The earliest known human settlements in Norway date to roughly 10,000 BCE. Numerous indigenous tribes lived in the area before being followed by Germanic tribes, especially the Vikings, who had a major impact on Norway's history and culture.

Viking Age (8th–11th century): The Viking Age is a significant era in the history of Norway. The Norwegian Vikings were well-known for their commerce, exploration, and seamanship abilities. In addition to other regions of Europe, they built communities in the British Isles, Iceland, Greenland, and even travelled as far as North America. Norway and the neighboring areas were profoundly impacted by Viking culture and influence.

Union with Denmark (late 14th to early 19th centuries): In the Kalmar Union, which took place in the late 14th century, Norway joined forces with Denmark. Throughout the many decades that this union existed, Norway progressively lost its political independence and became closer to Denmark.

Union with Sweden (1814–1905): In 1814, the Treaty of Kiel transferred control of Norway from Denmark to Sweden during the Napoleonic Wars. There was a brief era of freedom from 1814 to 1905 as a result of Norway's attempt to assert its independence and the enactment of a constitution. Norway peacefully ended its union with Sweden in 1905 and proclaimed itself a sovereign nation.

World Wars and the Modern Era: During World War I, Norway remained neutral, but during World War II, it was conquered by Nazi Germany. The nation was greatly impacted by the occupation, which lasted from 1940 to 1945. Following the war, Norway's economy grew quickly, in great part due to its petroleum resources. Norway became a wealthy country as a result of the late 1960s North Sea oil and gas discovery.
Norwegian society now

Norway has concentrated on preserving a robust welfare state, advancing social equality, and fostering sustainable development in recent decades.

The nation has actively participated in peacekeeping operations, environmental campaigns, and foreign diplomacy. With large expenditures in hydropower, wind power, and electric transportation, Norway is renowned for its dedication to sustainable energy.

This is merely a basic summary of Norway's history; there are many additional facts and occasions that have influenced the country. Please feel free to inquire if you have any special queries or would like more information about a particular historical era.

1.3 Traditions and Culture

The history, geography, and traditions of Norway are strongly ingrained in its culture and traditions. The following are some significant facets of Norwegian culture:

Values and Social Structure: Egalitarianism, equality, and social welfare are highly valued by Norwegians. Fairness, integrity, and respect for others are valued in society. People often respect one another equally regardless of socioeconomic rank because of the relatively flat social structure.

Norway's breathtaking natural landscapes play a key part in the culture of the nation. Norwegians value the outdoors and take part in activities like hiking, skiing, fishing, and camping. Spending time outside and appreciating nature are stressed by the idea of "friluftsliv" (open-air living).

Sami Culture: Norway's indigenous Sami population has a unique cultural history. They speak their own language, follow their own customs, and subsist off reindeer. Important cultural expressions include Sami handicrafts, traditional attire, and joik (a type of traditional music).

Festivals and Holidays: Throughout the year, Norwegians observe a variety of festivals and holidays. The most significant national holiday, National Day (May 17), commemorates the adoption of the Norwegian Constitution. Christmas, Easter, and Midsummer's Eve are a few other major holidays. Norway's culture and arts are celebrated annually at events including St. Olav's Festival, Bergen International Festival, and the Northern Lights Festival in Troms.

Food: Locally produced items, such as fish, seafood, game meat, berries, and root vegetables, are frequently used in traditional Norwegian cooking. Popular foods include "lutefisk," which is lye-soaked dried cod, "smoked salmon," "klippfisk," which is dried salted cod, "rakfisk," which is fermented fish, and "frikl," which is a stew of lamb and cabbage. Additionally loved are Norwegian dairy delicacies like brunost (brown cheese) and "rmmegrt" (sour cream porridge).

Art, Literature, and Music: Norway has made contributions to music, painting, sculpture, and literature. Significant literary contributions have been made by Norwegian writers including Sigrid Undset, Knut Hamsun, and Henrik Ibsen. One of the most well-known artists from Norway is Edvard Munch, who is best known for his classic picture "The Scream." Traditional Norwegian music consists of folk songs, fiddle tunes, and dances like the "Halling" and "Springar."

Norwegians often cherish their privacy and personal space. They respect others' time and value timeliness. To enter someone's home, one must take their shoes off. In Norway, tips are less frequent because most bills contain service costs.

Janteloven: The term "Janteloven" refers to a cultural idea that encourages modesty and disfavors individual bragging or exceptionalism. It elevates group cohesion while downplaying individual accomplishments. Even if Janteloven's impact has lessened over time, several areas of Norwegian culture still bear its imprint.

It's vital to remember that people and places in Norway can have different cultures and customs. There may be changes and deviations from what is described in this overview.

1.4 Weather and Climate

The weather and climate in Norway vary greatly throughout its enormous geographic area. The climate of the nation is a mixture of coastal, mountainous, and arctic. The climatic zones of Norway are shown below:
coastal regions in the west and south:

A temperate marine climate prevails along western and southern Norway's coasts. The average winter temperature ranges from 0°C to 7°C (32°F to 45°F), making it a comparatively pleasant season.

Temperatures in the summer range from 12°C to 20°C (54°F to 68°F), making them cold to pleasant. These areas see heavy annual precipitation, with the wettest months often falling in the late fall and early winter.

Northern and Inland Regions: Norway's northern and interior regions experience subarctic and arctic weather. Compared to the coastal regions, these locations have colder winters and cooler summers. In the winter, especially in the inland and northernmost locations, temperatures can drop dramatically, ranging from -10°C to -30°C (14°F to -22°F) or even lower. Inland regions often experience warm summers with temperatures between 10°C and 18°C (50°F and 64°F).

Alpine climate can be found in Norway's hilly areas like the Hardangervidda and Jotunheimen. Particularly during the winter, these regions receive cooler temperatures and more snowfall. Mountain tops are frequently covered with snow for much of the year, and altitude makes the climate more severe. Northern Lights: The most northern parts of Norway, such as Troms and Finnmark, provide the chance to see the Aurora Borealis, a mesmerizing natural phenomena. The winter season, from late September to early April, when the evenings are longer and darker, is the greatest time to see the Northern Lights.

It's crucial to remember that weather patterns can be unpredictable and that changes in precipitation and temperature can occur both within and between geographical regions. It's a good idea to research local climate and weather forecasts before traveling to a particular location or at a particular time.

1.5 The Perfect Period to Go

The activities you want to do and the areas you want to visit will determine when is the best time to visit Norway. When deciding on the ideal time to visit Norway, keep the following things in mind:
Summer (June through August)

In Norway, especially in the coastal areas, the summer is the busiest travel season. Temperatures in most places range from 10°C to 20°C (50°F to 68°F) due to the comparatively moderate weather. It's a perfect time to engage in outdoor pursuits like hiking, biking, fishing, and fjord exploration.

Additionally, the days grow longer, with some locations experiencing up to 24 hours of daylight.

December to March:
If you're interested in winter sports like skiing, snowboarding, or dog sledding, winter is a great time to visit Norway. During this time, there is also a chance to see the Northern Lights in Norway's northern regions. But there are times when the weather can be dreadful, with lows below zero and heavy snowfall.

(May and September) Shoulder Seasons:
In Norway, the shoulder seasons are from May and September. During these months, the weather is typically moderate and there are fewer tourists than during the summer. The fjords, national parks, and other outdoor attractions are ideal places to travel at this time. However, during this time, several tourist attractions can be closed.

It's also important to keep in mind that Norway's climate and weather can vary from one place to another and from year to year. It's a good idea to research local climate and weather forecasts before traveling to a particular location or at a particular time.

Planning a Trip to Norway

2.1 Passport and visa Requirements

Depending on your nationality, the itinerary, and the length of your stay, you may need a visa and passport to enter Norway. Here are some general guidelines for Norway's passport and visa requirements:

Every traveler to Norway needs to have a current passport. Your passport must be valid for at least six months after the day you intend to leave Norway. Make sure your passport has blank pages for immigration stamps.
Visa prerequisites:

Depending on your nationality, you may or may not need a visa to enter Norway. Norway is a party to the Schengen Agreement, which permits unrestricted travel among 26 European nations. A valid national identity card or passport is all you need to enter Norway if you are a citizen of a Schengen Area countries; a visa is not necessary.
You might need to apply for a Schengen visa ahead of time if you are not a citizen of a Schengen Area

nation. With a Schengen visa, you are able to travel to Norway and other Schengen nations for tourism, business, or other specific reasons for up to 90 days out of every 180. The Norwegian embassy or consulate in your home country is where you can submit an application for a Schengen visa.

No-Visa Travel:

For brief stays in Norway, certain nationals are free from needing a visa. These nations include numerous in Europe as well as the United States, Canada, Australia, New Zealand, Japan, and South Korea and many more European countries. These nationals don't need a visa to enter Norway or to stay there for up to 90 days within a 180-day period. However, as exceptions may differ, it's crucial to confirm the precise visa requirements based on your nationality.

Long-Term Work and Residency Visas:

You might need to apply for a different kind of visa or permission if you want to stay in Norway for longer than 90 days, work there, or study there. Work permits, student visas, and long-term stay visas all have unique restrictions and application procedures. For thorough information on the visa and permission requirements for your particular circumstances, it is advised that you get in touch with the Norwegian embassy or consulate that is most convenient for you in your country.

2.2 Money and Currency Issues

The Norwegian Krone (NOK) is the official currency of Norway. Here are some details about money and currency when traveling to Norway:
Change of Currencies:

It is recommended to convert your money into Norwegian Krone before traveling to Norway. You can do this through banks, exchange bureaus, or through legitimate online exchange services. In Norway, there are typically currency exchange services available at airports and in large cities.

ATMs:
Norway has several ATMs (Automated Teller Machines), which can be found at airports, cities, and towns. You can get Norwegian Krone out of an ATM using your debit or credit card. Make sure your card is approved for use abroad by contacting your bank in advance, and find out whether there are

any additional fees or charges for using an ATM abroad.

Credit cards:
Norway accepts credit cards like Visa and Mastercard widely, particularly in hotels, restaurants, shops, and bigger establishments. Smaller businesses or rural locations could favor cash payments. Nevertheless, it is wise to always have some cash on hand as a safety net.

Paying Procedures:
Norway is renowned for having a cashless economy and a large use of electronic payment systems. Transactions frequently involve contactless payment, smartphone payment apps (like Vipps), and chip-enabled cards. It is important to keep in mind that some businesses, particularly those in rural regions, might not accept credit cards, so having a modest bit of cash on you can be helpful.

Tipping:
Norway does not practice or anticipate tipping as frequently as some other nations. If you are happy with the service, it is traditional to round up the total or offer a little tip of 5–10%. In restaurants, the bill

typically includes a service fee. There is no
requirement to tip; it is completely optional.

VAT: Value-Added Tax
Value Added Tax (VAT) is used in Norway. If they
meet specific requirements, visitors from outside the
European Union (EU) are entitled to a VAT refund
on items purchased in Norway. To get a refund
before leaving the country, keep your receipts and
ask about the Tax-Free Shopping program at the
airport.

Security and Safety:
When it comes to financial matters, Norway is
typically a safe place. However, it is always
essential to take the usual security measures to
protect your possessions, such as watching your
wallet, using secure ATMs, and not flashing big
amounts of cash in public.
In order to prevent any problems with card
transactions being detected as suspicious activity,
keep in mind to let your bank or credit card provider
know about your travel plans to Norway.
To make sure you have the most current and correct
information, it is crucial to examine the most recent

currency conversion rates, fees, and other financial facts before your trip.

2.3 Travel Insurance

Travel insurance is strongly advised for anyone visiting Norway or any other country. In the event of unforeseen circumstances or emergencies while you are traveling, travel insurance offers you financial security and peace of mind. Here are some crucial considerations for travel insurance:

Medical Protection:
Medical expenses, such as those for hospitalization, emergency care, and even evacuation, are frequently covered by travel insurance. This is crucial if you experience any mishaps, diseases, or unanticipated medical issues while traveling.

Trip Abrupture or Cancellation:
If you need to cancel or shorten your vacation for a covered cause, such as illness, injury, or unforeseen circumstances, travel insurance can help you get reimbursed for non-refundable costs. It can assist you in recovering pre-paid expenses for travel, lodging, and other pre-arranged plans.

Baggage lost or delayed:

Baggage loss, theft, and delay are frequently covered by travel insurance. In the event that your luggage is delayed or misplaced by the airline or other transportation service, it may provide reimbursement for critical expenditures like clothing and toiletries.

Personal Responsibility

Personal liability coverage, which may be a part of your travel insurance, can safeguard you in the event that you unintentionally harm someone else or damage their property.

Services for Emergency Assistance:

Numerous travel insurance plans provide 24-hour emergency help. When you need quick assistance, such as for legal advice, medical referrals, or the organization of emergency medical evacuations, this can be quite helpful.

Adventure Activity Coverage:

Make sure your travel insurance policy covers adventure activities like skiing, snowboarding, hiking, or water sports if you want to partake in them. Due to their higher risk nature, some activities may be excluded or require supplementary coverage.

Study the Policy Specifics:
Read the policy terms, including coverage limitations, exclusions, and any necessary deductibles, thoroughly before acquiring travel insurance. Make sure the policy's terms and conditions match your unique needs by understanding them.

Earlier Medical Conditions:
Check your travel insurance policy to see if it covers pre-existing medical issues. Pre-existing condition coverage may be excluded from some policies or offered with restrictions.

Comparing insurance companies
Consider comparing coverage options, prices, and customer reviews by requesting quotes from many insurance companies. Look for reliable insurance providers with a solid history of processing claims and offering customer service.
While traveling, don't forget to carry a copy of your travel insurance policy and emergency contact information.

It's crucial to thoroughly evaluate your travel insurance requirements and pick a plan that fits your unique demands and the purpose of your trip to Norway.

2.4 Communication and Language

Norwegian (Norsk), specifically the Bokml standard written form, is the official language of Norway. While Sámi is acknowledged as an official language in some regions, Norway also boasts a number of regional dialects.

Here are some details on Norwegian language and communication:
English language ability
The majority of Norwegians are fluent in English, especially the younger generations and those employed in the tourism sector. You can anticipate finding English-speaking employees who can help you at well-known tourist attractions, motels, restaurants, and hotels.

Norwegian Expressions:
Despite the fact that English is a common language, learning a few fundamental Norwegian words can be beneficial and welcomed by locals. Here are a few typical sayings:

Hello: God dag (formally), Hei (informally).
I'm grateful. Takk
Yes: Ja
No: Nei
I'm sorry, Unnskyld meg
Are you an English speaker?Do you speak English?
Printed Material:

The majority of written material is available in both Norwegian and English, including menus, traffic signs, and signs for public transportation. You can find information boards, brochures, and maps in English in popular tourist destinations and large towns.

Centers for Tourist Information:
In Norway, tourist information centers often have staff members who are fluent in English and can assist with questions about travel, maps, and brochures. They can provide advice on activities, travel, and events in the area.

Tools for translation and mobile apps:
You can speak with locals or comprehend written Norwegian content if you need help translating

using one of the many mobile apps or online translation resources that are accessible.

Sign Languages:
The official sign language used by Norway's deaf community is called Norwegian Sign Language (NSL). However, English is typically a more accessible language for people who use sign language.

Respect for the regional tongue:
Visitors who make an effort to learn a few simple Norwegian phrases are appreciated by the Norwegians. Greeting people in Norwegian with words like "hello" and "thank you" can improve interactions and broaden your horizons.

Overall, as English is widely spoken and understood, language shouldn't be a major obstacle when visiting Norway. But it never hurts to brush up on a few fundamental words and learn to be sensitive to other cultures by respecting their languages and traditions.

2.5 Accommodation Options

Norway provides a variety of lodging choices to accommodate all tastes and price ranges. The following are some typical lodging options you might find in Norway:

2.5.1 Hotels

Hotels in Norway offer a variety of amenities and services to suit a wide range of budgets. Here are some details on hotels in Norway:

Various Hotel Types:
Norway offers a range of lodging choices, including family-run inns, boutique hotels, and global hotel brands. Hotels can be found all around the country in significant cities, small towns, and well-liked tourist locations.

Amount of stars
In Norway, hotels are often rated according to their degree of comfort and services using a star rating system. One star (for minimal lodgings) to five stars (for luxurious facilities) are the different star ratings. Hotels with higher ratings typically provide more

facilities, roomy accommodations, and extra services.

Services and Amenities:
Hotels in Norway provide a variety of extras and services, such as:
Each room has an ensuite bathroom with towels and supplies.
Internet or Wi-Fi access
minibars, televisions, and in-room safes
daily housekeeping as well as room service
Local eateries and bars
Swimming pools, fitness centers, or spa services
Meeting spaces and conferences for business travelers
Concierge services can help with booking trips, making recommendations, and gathering local knowledge

Breakfast:
In many hotels in Norway, breakfast is included in the nightly charge. A buffet of foods, such as bread, cheese, cold cuts, eggs, cereals, yogurt, fruits, and beverages, is a common feature of Norwegian breakfasts. It's important to make sure breakfast is included when booking a hotel.

Reserving and Booking:

It is suggested to make your hotel reservations in advance, especially during busy travel times or if you have specialized requirements. You may compare costs, read reviews, and book hotels using online travel portals, hotel booking services, and official hotel websites.

Payment:

Major credit cards are typically accepted by hotels in Norway. However, it's a good idea to find out in advance whether the hotel accepts your chosen means of payment. Upon check-in, certain hotels could want a credit card authorization or a deposit.

Location:

Hotels can be found all around Norway, including in city centers, close to tourist sites, on the coast, and in picturesque rural locations. Based on your travel schedule and the pursuits you want to make, think about where you want to stay.

Accessibility:

It is advised to speak with the hotel directly if you have specific accessibility needs, such as wheelchair accessibility or special accommodations, to learn more about their services and facilities for visitors with disabilities.

Don't forget to review each hotel's individual policies and conditions, especially those pertaining to cancellations, check-in and check-out times, and any additional fees or penalties.
You can choose a suitable hotel in Norway to improve your vacation experience by taking into account your preferences, spending limit, and preferred location.

Suitable Hotels
Oslo's The Thief
Location: Oslo, 0252 Landgangen 1
An upscale hotel in Oslo that is close to the water. It has chic accommodations, a gallery, a rooftop patio, a spa, and a highly regarded restaurant.
Website address: thethief.com

Hotel Continental Oslo :
Location: 0117 Oslo, Stortingsgata 24/26
An exquisite and historic hotel located in the center of Oslo. It has cozy accommodations, a well-known bistro, a piano bar, and convenient access to popular attractions.

Visit the hotelcontinental.no website.

Lofthus's Hotel Ullensvang (Hardangerfjord):
Address: 14 Tyssedalsvegen, 5787 Lofthus
Family-friendly motel offering breathtaking views of the Hardangerfjord and neighboring mountains. It offers a variety of activities, plush accommodations, a spa, and swimming pools.
Visit the hotel-ullensvang.no website.

Oslo's Scandic Holmenkollen Park:
In Oslo, at Kongeveien 26, 0787.
A historic hotel with sweeping views of Oslo is located in the picturesque Holmenkollen neighborhood. It has cozy accommodations, a spa, a pool, and is close to skiing and other outdoor activities.
Internet address: https://www.scandichotels.com/hotels/norway/oslo/scandic-holmenkollen-park

Hotel Radisson Blu Royal (Bergen):
Location: 5003 Bryggen, Bergen
A contemporary hotel is situated in Bergen's famed Bryggen neighborhood. It features chic

accommodations, a rooftop patio, a fitness facility, and a prime position near landmarks and the lake.
Visit the following website: www.radissonhotels.com/en-us/hotels/radisson-blu-bergen

Please be aware that these suggestions are supported by reviews and general goodwill. When picking a hotel, it's wise to do your homework, read recent reviews, evaluate rates, and take into account your own preferences and needs.

2.5.2 Suggested Hotels

Oslo's Anker Hostel:
Storgata 55, 0182 Oslo is the location.
A well-known hostel offering a variety of private and dormitory accommodations in the heart of Oslo. It offers a bar, a 24-hour front desk, a communal kitchen, and laundry facilities.
URL of website: www.ankerhostel.no

Budget hotel in Bergen (Bergen):
Location: 5017 Bergen, Kong Oscars Gate 45
Located in Bergen's city center and adjacent to the well-known Bryggen neighborhood, this hostel is

reasonably priced. It features private and shared dormitory rooms, free Wi-Fi, a communal kitchen, and a laid-back ambiance.
Internet address: www.bergenbudgethotel.no

Oslo's Haraldsheim Hostel:
Address: Haraldsheimveien 4, Oslo, 0587
Located in a peaceful neighborhood of Oslo, this hostel offers both private rooms and dorm beds at reasonable prices. It has a garden, a café, outdoor seats, and a shared kitchen.
Website address: haraldsheim.no

In Stavanger, at St. Svithun Vandrerhjem:
Location: 4008 Stavanger, Madlaveien 35
A variety of private rooms and dormitories are available at this hostel, which is located close to Stavanger's city center. It offers a garden, a café, a communal kitchen, and quick access to well-liked attractions.
Visit the following website: stavanger-stsvithun.no

(Trondheim) Trondheim Vandrerhjem
Location: 7043 Trondheim, Weidemannsvei 41
Located close to the city center of Trondheim, this hostel provides budget-friendly dorm and private

rooms. It has a welcoming ambiance, a shared kitchen, a cozy lounge, and laundry facilities.
the website trondheimvandrerhjem.no

Please be aware that these suggestions are supported by reviews and general goodwill. When selecting a hostel, it's wise to do your homework, read recent reviews, evaluate rates, and take into account your own preferences and needs.

2.5.3 Recommendations for Guesthouse

Hotel Solstrand & Bad (Os):
Location: 5200 Os Solstrandveien 200
In close proximity to Bergen, a historic inn may be found on the Bjrnefjord's shoreline. There are gorgeous guest rooms, lovely gardens, a spa, a private beach, and expansive views of the fjord available.
www.solstrand.com is the website address.
English Grammar (Tjme)
The address is Engveien 227, 3145 Time.
On a little island close to Oslo, there is a charming guesthouse. It offers a relaxing and opulent experience with chic guest rooms, a spa, a beach, gardens, and a farm-to-table restaurant.

URL of website: www.engogard.no

Hotel Juvet Landscape in Valldal:
Location: 6210 Valldal, Alstad
Described as a distinctive inn with minimalist, contemporary construction that merges with the landscape, the guesthouse is tucked away in the beautiful Norwegian countryside. It offers guests custom built accommodations, a riverside spa, and outdoor recreation options.
URL of website: www.juvet.com

Reine Rorbuer (Lofoten Islands: Reine):
Location: 8390 Reine in Reine.
A group of historic fishing huts that have been transformed into guesthouses are located in the charming settlement of Reine in the Lofoten Islands. It provides comfortable lodging, breathtaking scenery, and straightforward access to hiking, fishing, and Northern Lights observations.
Web address: reinerorbuer.no

(Lyngen Alps) Lyngen Lodge
Location: 9060 Lyngseidet, Nord-Lenangen
A isolated inn in the Lyngen Alps offers a blend of contemporary comfort and wilderness adventure. It

offers warm lodgings, a sauna, outdoor pursuits like skiing and hiking, and spectacular views of the mountains and fjords in the region.
Website address: lyngenlodge.com

Please be aware that these suggestions are supported by reviews and general goodwill. When selecting a guesthouse, it's wise to do your homework, read recent reviews, evaluate pricing, and take into account your own preferences and needs.

2.5.4 Recommendations for Airbnb and other Accommodation types

Here are a few reputable websites for Airbnb and holiday rentals in Norway where you may find a wide choice of possibilities, though I can't speak to current information or personal preferences in real time:
Website: www.airbnb.com
In Norway, Airbnb provides a range of holiday rental choices, including condos, homes, cabins, and distinctive lodgings. Rentals can be found using location, dates, and particular criteria. To make sure a listing fits your demands, it is essential to read the descriptions, comments, and ratings of each one.

Website for booking.com

Booking.com provides a large range of vacation rentals, including apartments, houses for rent, and cabins in different parts of Norway, in addition to hotel reservations. You may read visitor testimonials, compare pricing, and filter results using the website.

Web site: www.homeaway.com

Vacation rentals in Norway are available on HomeAway, a member of the Vrbo family, and include cabins, cottages, and homes. In order to select the ideal rental property, it offers a user-friendly search tool that enables you to specify your ideal location, vacation dates, and facilities

.

(www.expedia.com) Expedia

You can search for and reserve vacation rentals in Norway on Expedia, including condos, houses, and cabins. The platform offers thorough property information, images, customer testimonials, and a safe booking procedure.

Visit Tripadvisor at www.tripadvisor.com.

Popular travel website Tripadvisor features vacation rental reviews in addition to hotel reviews. There are many different rental alternatives available, including apartments, Norwegian houses, and cottages. Before making a reservation, you have the option to read reviews, see pictures, and compare pricing.

Check the property specifics, amenities, cancellation restrictions, and any additional fees related to the rental while using these platforms. Before confirming your reservation, it's also a good idea to get in touch with the host or property owner to ask any questions or address any issues you may have.

Please be aware that in order to guarantee a seamless and pleasurable vacation rental experience, it is crucial to book through reliable sites, check reviews from prior visitors, and connect directly with the property owner or host.

2.6 Modes of transportation

2.6.1 Air Travel

Given the abundance of domestic and international airports in Norway, flying is a practical alternative for both domestic travel and international arrivals. Here are some details on air travel in Norway: important airports

Oslo Airport, Gardermoen (OSL): The largest airport in Norway and a significant international gateway, it is situated in Gardermoen, close to Oslo. The second-busiest airport in Norway, Bergen Airport, Flesland (BGO), is located close to Bergen and provides a wide range of domestic and international connections.

The Stavanger Airport in Sola, Norway (SVG), is a prominent airport for both domestic and international travel, mainly for trips involving the oil sector.

Trondheim Airport, Vaernes (TRD): This significant airport in central Norway is located at Vrnes, close to Trondheim, and it provides a range of local and international flights.

Internal Flights:
Several airlines, including SAS (Scandinavian Airlines), Norwegian Air Shuttle, Widere, and Norwegian regional carriers run domestic flights

within Norway. It is convenient to travel around Norway with these airlines' flights to Norway's major cities, towns, and rural locations.

Flying internationally:
Norway has regular flights from major carriers to Oslo Airport, Gardermoen, connecting it to a number of worldwide locations. SAS, Norwegian Air Shuttle, Lufthansa, British Airways, KLM, Air France, and many other well-known airlines fly to and from Norway. There are direct flights from a number of European cities as well as North America, Asia, and other locations.

Facilities at airports:
Airports in Norway provide a variety of amenities and services, including check-in desks, luggage handling, security screenings, duty-free stores, dining options, car rental options, and connections to public transportation. Particularly the Gardermoen terminal at Oslo Airport offers a wide variety of services, such as lounges, shopping spaces, and food choices.

Getting to and from airports:

In general, city centers and other places are easily accessible from Norwegian airports. Airport express trains, buses, taxis, and rental cars are some of the available modes of transit to and from the airports. Additionally, several airports provide private transports and shuttle services.

Check-in and security

Passengers flying to or from Norway must pass through security screenings and abide by all policies established by the airline and airport authorities, just as with any other foreign flight. It is wise to be to the airport plenty of time before your flight is scheduled to take off in order to allow for check-in, security screenings, and any potential unanticipated delays.

To get the greatest deals, it's advised to check flight availability, compare costs, and reserve your tickets well in advance of your trip. Review the permitted amount of luggage, any additional conditions or limitations, and become familiar with the airline's policies and procedures.

It's always a good idea to check with the relevant airlines and airports for the most recent information before your trip as timetables, routes, and policies for air travel may change.

2.6.2 Railroads

In Norway, trains are a common and effective method of transportation, providing beautiful routes and practical links between towns and regions. Here are some details on Norwegian train travel:

Countrywide Rail Service:
The company Vy, formerly known as NSB (Norges Statsbaner), runs Norway's national rail service. Regular train service is provided by Vy to all major cities and communities in the nation. The comfort, reliability, and breathtaking views of Norway's landscapes are hallmarks of the trains.

Railroad Routes:
Norway's rail system links a number of cities and regions, with some of the most well-traveled routes including:
The Bergen Line, which runs from Oslo to Bergen, is among the world's most picturesque train routes and provides breath-taking views of mountains, fjords, and waterfalls.

The Dovre Line offers a scenic ride through forests and valleys from Oslo to Trondheim.

The Nordland Line travels from Trondheim to Bod, passing over the Arctic Circle and showing the untamed scenery of northern Norway.

The Srland Line offers a travel from Oslo to Stavanger through the southern coastal districts, passing through quaint towns and picturesque coastal vistas.

Facilities and comforts:

Norwegian trains provide various service classes, including normal class and occasionally a first-class alternative. The trains have soft seats, lots of legroom, space for luggage, power outlets, and free Wi-Fi. There may be dining cars or a trolley service that provides food and refreshments on some long-distance trains.

Bookings and Tickets:

To guarantee a seat, it is advised to purchase train tickets in advance, especially for lengthy and well-traveled lines. You can buy tickets at train stations or online on the Vy website. Except for some picturesque routes and overnight services, reservations are normally not needed for domestic trains.

Rail Tickets:
Consider a Eurail Pass or Interrail Pass if you intend to use frequent trains both inside of Norway and maybe to neighboring nations. These passes provide flexible travel alternatives. With these tickets, you can ride several trains simultaneously. However, keep in mind that additional bookings for seats on some trains might be necessary and are dependent on availability.

Railway Stations
Major cities' train stations are well-stocked with amenities like ticket booths, self-service kiosks, waiting lounges, and occasionally stores and cafes. The principal rail hub is Oslo Central Station (Oslo S), and central stations are also located in Bergen, Trondheim, and Stavanger.
Scenic Train Trips

The picturesque lines of Norway's train system, which provide breath-taking vistas of mountains, fjords, and waterfalls, are well-known. For instance, the Flm Railway is a well-liked tourist destination that offers a breathtaking journey between Myrdal and Flm over rugged mountains and lovely valleys.

When planning your rail travel in Norway, please keep in mind that train timetables, routes, and ticket costs might vary, so it's always advised to check the Vy website or other trustworthy sources for the most recent information.

2.6.3 Buses

Buses are a practical and economical means of transportation within Norway, particularly for getting to smaller towns, distant locations, and picturesque routes. Here are some details on bus travel in Norway:

a bus company

In Norway, a number of bus companies provide both local and long-distance bus services. Nor-Way Bussekspress, Vy Express, Nettbuss, and Flybussen are a few of Norway's well-known bus operators. There may be different routes, schedules, and ticketing procedures for every firm.

Local and regional buses:

Within particular Norwegian towns and regions, transportation is provided by regional and local buses. These buses are a great choice for visiting smaller cities, towns, and tourist destinations that are not reachable by train. They follow set routes and frequently make several stops along the way.

Buses for Long Distances:

Long-distance buses connect Norway's major cities and towns, providing a more inexpensive option than taking the train. These buses offer cozy seating, space for bags, and occasionally extras like Wi-Fi and power outlets. For longer trips, certain long-distance buses also provide overnight services.

Dedicated bus routes:

Express bus lines are well-liked for getting about between big cities and areas. For instance, the express bus services "Nor-Way Bussekspress" and "Vy Express" link a number of locations, including Oslo, Bergen, Stavanger, Trondheim, and other places.

Routes for scenic buses:
Norway is renowned for its breathtaking landscapes, and there are several scenic bus routes that let you take in the splendor of the nation's surroundings. The "National Tourist Routes" include bus routes, for instance, that travel via breathtaking fjords, mountains, and coastal regions.

Bookings and Tickets:
Typically, bus tickets can be bought at bus stops, online through the website of the bus company, or occasionally, straight from the driver. For long distance trips, it is best to purchase tickets in advance, especially during the busiest travel times. Some bus companies also provide smartphone apps for electronic ticketing and ticket purchasing.

Facilities and bus stops:
In larger cities, bus stations often offer amenities including ticket booths, waiting areas, restrooms, and occasionally cafes or stores. Bus stops are places where you wait for the bus to arrive in smaller towns. It is advised to get to the bus stop or station a few minutes before the departure time.
Rural regions and far-off locations

In isolated and rural areas of Norway, where train service may be constrained or nonexistent, buses are frequently the main mode of transportation. These buses serve the local population and offer transportation to neighboring cities, towns, and tourist destinations.

Tickets and travel passes that can be combined:
For several bus trips within a given area or time period, some bus companies offer combination tickets or travel cards. If you want to spend a lot of time exploring a particular place, they can be affordable choices.

When planning your bus travel in Norway, please keep in mind that bus schedules, routes, and ticket costs can change. It is therefore advised to visit the bus company's website or get in touch with the local tourist information office for the most recent information.

2.6.4 Rental cars and excellent services in Norway

You can explore Norway at your own pace with the ease and flexibility of car rentals in Norway. Here are some details on automobile rentals in Norway and suggested rental agencies:

Companies that rent cars:
In Norway, there are a number of reputable domestic and international automobile rental firms. Popular examples include:
Avis
The Hertz
the Europcar
The Sixt
Finances (www.budget.com)
www.enterprise.com, the company.
Rental prerequisites:

In Norway, you normally need to fulfill the following conditions:
Age: Although it may vary depending on the rental business, the minimum age limit is typically 21 years old. Drivers under the age of 25 might be charged extra fees.

Driving Permit: A current driving permit from your native country is usually adequate. Most nationalities do not require international driving licences, however they might be helpful as an additional form of identification.

reserving and booking:

It's a good idea to reserve your rental car in advance, especially during periods of high travel demand, to ensure availability and lock in the most competitive prices. Online reservations are frequently made through the rental company's website or trusted third-party travel websites. It is advised to shop about, study the fine print, and look for any hidden costs or restrictions.

Insurance and rental rates:
The cost of renting a car varies based on the rental agency, the type of vehicle, how long the rental is, and any additional services. The cost of renting a vehicle usually includes basic insurance coverage, however it is advised to look into better insurance choices, such collision damage waiver (CDW) and theft protection. It is crucial to read the rental agreement in its entirety and comprehend the insurance coverage, deductibles, and any exclusions.

Rental Return and Pickup:

There are pick-up and drop-off places for car rentals at significant airports, in urban areas, and at other designated rental offices. One-way rentals, which let you pick up and drop off the vehicle at different locations, could be an option offered by some rental agencies. Make sure you are familiar with the rental company's fueling procedures, mileage restrictions, and any additional fees for damage or late returns.

Conditions on the roads and traffic laws:

Norway has well-maintained roads, however some areas, especially those that are isolated or in mountains, may have roads that are curvy or narrow. Driving safely is crucial, as is adhering to traffic laws and speed restrictions. If you intend to travel during the winter, make sure your rental car has the proper winter tires installed, or think about renting a car with studded tires. Winter driving conditions can be difficult.

Services for recommended car rentals:

The following vehicle rental companies have earned favorable evaluations in Norway: Avis, Hertz, Europcar, Sixt, Budget, and Enterprise, albeit I don't have access to real-time information. But before choosing a rental agency, it's always a good idea to check prices, read user reviews, and take into account the particular needs of your trip.

It's vital to examine the precise terms and conditions of your selected rental business and remain current with local traffic rules and regulations while planning your car rental in Norway because driving legislation, road conditions, and rental policies are subject to change.

2.6.5 Ferries

Ferries play a significant role in Norwegian transportation, especially for trips along the coast and to the numerous islands that make up the nation. The following details ferry transport in Norway:

Beach Ferries:
Numerous ferry lines connect Norway's coastal regions, providing scenic and practical transportation alternatives. These ferries link different ports and give access to outlying settlements, fjords, and islands. The coastal ferries provide a distinctive opportunity to explore

Norway's natural beauty and are renowned for their breathtaking views of the country's coastline.

Ferries to Fjord:
The magnificent fjords of Norway can be explored by taking a fjord ferry. These ships travel along specialized fjord routes, giving you the opportunity to witness stunning vistas of craggy mountains, gushing waterfalls, and tranquil fjord settings. The Geirangerfjord, Sognefjord, Hardangerfjord, and Lysefjord are a few well-known fjord ferry routes.

Islands and a chain of islands:
Ferries are frequently the main mode of transportation to Norway's numerous islands and archipelagos, which line its coastlines. The Lofoten Islands, Vesterlen Islands, and Vega Archipelago are the most well-known archipelagos because they provide exceptional natural beauty and distinctive cultural experiences.

Ferry Companiess:
In Norway, there are numerous ferry companies that serve both vehicles and passengers. Hurtigruten, Fjord1, Norled, and Torghatten Nord are a few of the well-known boat operators. For the most recent

information, it's vital to visit the websites of the operators or get in touch with them directly as each one may have various routes, schedules, and facilities.

Plans and Tickets:
Depending on the route, the time of year, and the operator, ferry schedules can change. For the most up-to-date timetables and to reserve your tickets in advance, especially during seasons of high travel demand, check the ferry company's website or get in touch with their customer service. While some ferry companies allow you to purchase tickets online, others may insist that you do so at the port in person.
Infrastructure and Amenities:

The facilities and amenities offered on Norwegian ferries differ. Onboard cafes or restaurants, pleasant seating areas, restrooms, and outside viewing decks are common features of larger ferries. Despite having fewer amenities, smaller ships nonetheless offer basic seating and protection from the elements.
Passes and Tickets that Combine:
Some ferry companies provide combo tickets or passes that permit multiple ferry trips within a predetermined area or time frame. If you want to

travel to various islands or other coastal locations, these can be useful.

Island and Fjord Tours:

Specialized fjord and island tours, which offer guided excursions and commentary on the environmental and cultural features of particular places, are additionally offered to normal ferry services. These excursions provide a more comprehensive experience and are a wonderful opportunity to enjoy the natural beauty of Norway's coastal regions.

Please be aware that ferry times, routes, and ticket costs can change, particularly if unforeseeable events or low demand occur. When arranging your ferry trip in Norway, it is advised to visit the ferry operator's website or get in touch with them directly for the most recent information.

Norway's Regions and Cities

3.1 Oslo

Here is a description of Oslo, Norway's capital and largest city:

Geography and the Cityscape

Oslo is situated near the northern end of the Oslofjord on Norway's southern coast. Hills, forests, and lakes surround the city, creating a stunning natural background. Oslo boasts a compact city core that is simple to navigate on foot, as well as a mix of modern and old architecture.

Historical and Cultural Importance:

The cultural and historical legacy of Oslo is extensive. Since the 14th century, it has served as Norway's capital and has been an important part of its history. The city's numerous museums, art galleries, and historical sites serve to highlight its heritage.

landmarks and attractions

There are many sights and landmarks to discover in Oslo. Among the best ones are:

The Norwegian monarch's formal palace is located in the city center and is known as the Royal Palace.

The Norwegian National Opera and Ballet are housed in the magnificent Oslo Opera House.

Contains extremely well-preserved artifacts and ships from the Viking Age.

The Holmenkollen Ski Museum and Tower is a historic ski jump tower that offers breathtaking city views in addition to a museum devoted to the history of skiing.

The largest sculpture park in the world was built by a single artist, Gustav Vigeland, and is called the Vigeland Sculpture Park.

Akershus fortification is a historic medieval fortification and castle with stunning views of the city and fjord.

Garden Areas and Parks:

Oslo is renowned for its plethora of parks and outdoor recreation options. Several well-liked parks and open spaces are:

The Bygdy Peninsula is a picturesque peninsula with a number of museums and lovely walking paths.

Oslofjord: During the summer, boat rides, island hopping, and swimming are all possible in this fjord.

A park with sculptures, art installations, and vista points is called Ekeberg Park.

Nordmarka: An large forestland that surrounds Oslo and is great for hiking, skiing, and outdoor recreation.

Cultural Events and Life:
Oslo has a thriving cultural scene with many annual festivals, concerts, and events. The Nobel Peace Prize ceremony is held in the city at Oslo City Hall. You may also enjoy Norwegian art and culture in a number of theaters, music venues, and galleries.

Eating and cooking:
With a variety of international cuisines and traditional Norwegian dishes, Oslo has a thriving food scene. Seafood, reindeer, and traditional cured meats are among of the regional specialties. You may try Norwegian cuisine in the city's many eateries, cafes, and food markets.

Transportation:
Oslo has a reliable public transportation system that includes trains, buses, trams, and the metro (T-bane). With designated bike lanes and rental options, biking is also well-liked. Access to public

transportation is limitless, and many attractions are free to enter with the Oslo Pass.

Overall, Oslo offers a unique fusion of urban appeal, nature, culture, and history. No matter what your interests are—museum exploration, outdoor recreation, or experiencing Scandinavian city life—this city has much to offer.

3.1.1 Popular Destinations/Top Attractions

Some of Oslo's top sights are listed below:
Viking Ship Museum: This museum exhibits relics and displays linked to Viking culture and history, as well as exceptionally well-preserved Viking ships from the ninth century.

The largest sculpture park ever created by a single artist, Gustav Vigeland, is called the Vigeland Sculpture Park and is situated within Frogner Park. It contains more than 200 bronze and granite sculptures of the human body in a range of expressions.

Oslo Opera House: The Norwegian National Opera and Ballet are housed in this spectacular architectural monument. Visitors can stroll on the sloping roof thanks to its distinctive design, which provides panoramic views of both the city and the Oslofjord.

The waterfront location of the medieval fortress and castle complex known as Akershus Fortress provides a window into Oslo's past. Explore the grounds, tour the old castle, and take in the beautiful views of the city and fjord.

The Holmenkollen Ski Museum and Tower is a famous ski jump tower that doubles as a museum detailing the development of skiing in Norway. Visitors may discover more about the activity, take in the expansive views from the observation deck, and even experience a virtual ski jump.

Munch Museum: This museum showcases a sizable collection of Edvard Munch's paintings, including his most well-known piece, "The Scream." It is devoted to the works of the famed Norwegian painter.

The Royal Palace is an outstanding structure encircled by lovely gardens and parkland and serves as the official residence of the Norwegian monarch. The palace grounds are open to visitors, who may also see the guards changing.

National Gallery: This museum of fine arts is home to a sizable collection of Norwegian and foreign artwork, including pieces by Edvard Munch and other well-known artists including Pablo Picasso and Vincent van Gogh.

The Fram Museum, which is devoted to arctic exploration, the Kon-Tiki Museum, which highlights Thor Heyerdahl's expeditions, and the Norwegian Folk Museum, which showcases Norwegian cultural heritage, are all located on the Bygdy Peninsula, which is just outside the city center.
The Tjuvholmen neighborhood's Astrup Fearnley Museum of Modern Art is a museum of contemporary art that houses a collection of modern and contemporary works by Norwegian and foreign artists.

These sights give tourists a comprehensive view of Oslo's past, present, and future while also showcasing its stunning natural surroundings.

3.1.2 Best Places to Eat and Drink

A variety of eateries, cafes, and bars in Oslo cater to a wide range of tastes, making the city's culinary scene both active and diversified. Some of Oslo's top restaurants and bars are listed below:

Oslo's Mathallen is a food hall that is home to a variety of speciality food stores, cafes, and restaurants. It is situated in the Vulkan neighborhood. It's a wonderful place to discover and savor a variety of delectable foods, such as fresh seafood, cheeses, meats, pastries, and international cuisines.

Grünerlkka: This hip district is renowned for its thriving eating scene. Numerous cafes, restaurants, and pubs may be found here serving a variety of foreign, fusion, and regional delicacies. It's a terrific place to explore and find uncommon dining options.

Aker Brygge is a well-liked destination for dining and entertainment. It is located along the waterfront. It has a wide range of eateries and pubs serving anything from sushi and seafood to Italian and Mediterranean meals. It's a pleasant place to eat because of the picturesque harbor views.

Vulkan: A number of eateries and pubs can be found in the Vulkan neighborhood, which is close to Mathallen Oslo. It provides a variety of craft brews, exotic flavors, and cutting-edge eating concepts. It's a well-liked destination for foodies and those seeking a lively eating experience.

Torggata: This street in the heart of Oslo is renowned for its variety of food establishments. Torggata offers a variety of foods to suit every taste, including traditional Norwegian fare as well as Mexican, Japanese, and Middle Eastern cuisine.

Maaemo: Maaemo is a Michelin-starred restaurant in Oslo that specializes on displaying Norwegian ingredients and culinary traditions for a quality dining experience. It offers an exceptional tasting menu that is both unique and developed by well-known chefs.

Tim Wendelboe is a specialty coffee shop and micro-roastery in Grünerlkka that coffee aficionados shouldn't miss. They procure and roast their own beans, guaranteeing premium coffee that is expertly made.

Himkok: Regarded as one of Oslo's top cocktail bars, Himkok serves a variety of expertly created drinks that use ingredients that are acquired locally. Cocktail lovers and those seeking an unusual drinking experience frequent this location.

If you enjoy seafood, check out Vulkanfisk, a seafood bar and restaurant that offers mouthwateringly fresh fish meals. It's a terrific place to savor the coastal delicacies of Norway, from oysters to fish soups and classic Norwegian seafood platters.

Smalhans: Smalhans offers a seasonal menu with a focus on local products for a taste of contemporary Norwegian cuisine. The eatery is a popular choice for a laid-back dining experience because of its comfortable and casual ambiance.

These are just a few of the many wonderful eating alternatives Oslo has to offer. Oslo's food and drink culture has something to please every palate, whether you're seeking for traditional Norwegian fare, global cuisines, or cutting-edge culinary experiences.

3.1.3 Shopping

A variety of contemporary shopping malls, department stores, boutiques, and speciality shops can be found in Oslo. Here are some of Oslo's well-known shopping centers and districts:

Oslo's main thoroughfare, Karl Johans Gate, is a well-liked shopping area. Along its length, which runs from the Royal Palace to the Central Station, are a variety of upscale retailers, boutiques, department stores, and eateries. Along this busy boulevard, you may find both global names and regional designers.

Aker Brygge is a bustling neighborhood with a variety of stores, eateries, and cafes that is situated along the waterfront. It provides a mix of specialist shops, local fashion boutiques, and international brands. While shopping, you may take in the lovely harbor vistas and bustling environment.

Bogstadveien is one of Oslo's main shopping avenues, and it is located in the wealthy Majorstuen area. A variety of high-end apparel, designer boutiques, specialist shops, and well-known chain stores are available. There is a huge selection of clothing, accessories, home goods, and cosmetics available.

Grünerlkka: A district with a distinctive shopping environment, known for its hip and alternative attitude. There are numerous independent boutiques, vintage shops, and concept stores there that sell clothing, accessories, works of art, and other design-related goods. In this hip neighborhood, you can find unusual and diverse products.

As was already noted, the food hall Mathallen in Oslo houses a variety of speciality food stores. Along with the delicious foods, there are boutique shops where you can buy gourmet goods, specialty cookware, and other interesting food-related stuff.
Paleet is a premium shopping mall with a carefully chosen collection of high-end fashion and lifestyle companies. It is located on Karl Johans Gate. It provides a classy shopping experience with an emphasis on exclusivity and luxury.

Oslo City: One of Oslo's biggest shopping centers, Oslo City is situated near to the Central Station. It has many different types of stores, including those selling clothing, accessories, gadgets, books, and more. The mall also features a food court, eateries, and cafes.

Oslo has a vibrant vintage and secondhand market, with a number of shops selling distinctive apparel, accessories, furniture, and home decor. Pre-owned items can be found in abundance at stores like Fretex, Velouria Vintage, and Robot.

Farmers Markets: There are a number of farmers markets in Oslo where you can buy local, fresh vegetables, crafts, and artisanal goods. Mathallen's Farmers Market, Bondens Market, and Grnland Basar Farmers Market are a few examples.

Design and crafts: Oslo offers a number of shops and galleries that feature Norwegian and Nordic design goods for individuals who are interested in Scandinavian design and crafts. A carefully curated range of design products is available at stores like Norway Designs, Kunstindustrimuseet Shop, and Jannike Krkvik & Alessandro D'Orazio.

These are only a few instances of the shopping options Oslo offers. Oslo has something to offer any type of shopper, whether they enjoy high-end clothing, exclusive stores, regional goods, or Scandinavian design.

3 1.4 Best Places to Stay in Oslo

Here are some suggestions for lodging in Oslo that span many categories:

Luxury lodging
The Thief is a chic and opulent hotel on the water in Tjuvholmen. It has luxury accommodations, a rooftop patio, a spa, and a renowned restaurant.

The Hotel Continental is a traditional, upscale hotel located in the center of Oslo. The Royal Palace and Karl Johans Gate are nearby, and it has magnificent accommodations and a renowned seafood restaurant.

Midrange lodging:
Scandic Vulkan: Situated in the hip Vulkan neighborhood, this hotel provides contemporary accommodations, a rooftop bar with expansive city views, and convenient access to local eateries, stores, and attractions.

Saga Hotel Oslo Central: A boutique hotel in a prime position, next to Karl Johans Gate and the Central Station, with cozy rooms and a free breakfast buffet.

Cheap hotels:
Anker Hotel is a reasonably priced hotel close to Grünerlkka. It offers affordable, straightforward lodging with free breakfast and easy access to the lively eating and nightlife of the city.

Citybox Oslo is a low-cost hotel with reasonably priced, contemporary rooms. Self-check-in is available, and guests have access to amenities like a common kitchen and lounge.

Hostels:
Anker Hostel: This budget-friendly hostel is close to Grünerlkka and provides both private rooms and dorms. It contains a game room, a bar, and a community kitchen.

Oslo Hostel Central: This hostel offers convenient lodging at an affordable price in the heart of the city. It provides common cooking space in addition to private rooms and dormitories.

These are but a few suggestions; Oslo offers a wide range of lodging choices to match various spending ranges and tastes. Before making a reservation, it's always a good idea to check the property's availability, read reviews, and compare pricing to be sure your demands will be met.

3.1.5 Entertainment

The nightlife in Oslo is active and diversified, with a variety of alternatives to suit all tastes. Here are some of Oslo's most well-liked nightlife hot spots and locales:

Grünerlkka: This trendy area is well recognized for its exciting nightlife. There are numerous taverns, pubs, and clubs there that include a range of musical styles and ambiances. Grünerlkka offers something for everyone, from relaxed bars with live music to energetic dance clubs.

Aker Brygge is a well-liked destination for dining and entertainment. It is situated along the waterfront. It has a number of waterfront taverns, pubs, and clubs. Drinks can be enjoyed while looking out over the harbor, or you can dance the night away at one of the exciting clubs.

Karl Johans Gate: Karl Johans Gate, Oslo's major thoroughfare, is home to a number of bars, taverns, and clubs. A lot of places host DJ sets, karaoke nights, or live music events. People enjoying the lively environment fill the street at night.

Youngstorget: A square in the heart of the city that regularly holds events and concerts. It's also renowned for its vibrant pub scene, where a number of venues provide craft brews, cocktails, and live music.

Vulkan: The neighborhood of Vulkan, which is next to Grünerlkka, is renowned for its hip bars and clubs. It features a variety of electronic music, DJ performances, and themed parties and draws a younger demographic.

Rockefeller Music Hall is a well-known music venue in Oslo where both national and international performers play live concerts. It's a well-known location for music lovers to take in live performances in a lively setting.

Bl: This well-liked club and concert location, which is next to the Akerselva River, is renowned for its wide range of musical selections. Local bands and DJs provide live sets that include music from a variety of genres, including jazz, indie, techno, and more.

Revolver is a well-known underground club in the Grünerlkka district that is well-known for its alternative music culture. It holds a variety of events, such as themed parties, DJ sets, and live music performances.

Himkok: Although largely renowned for its cocktail bars, Himkok also has a thriving nightlife. It offers locally sourced ingredients for its artisan cocktails and frequently organizes DJ nights and live entertainment.

Oslo Opera House: The Oslo Opera House not only has cultural value, but it also has a distinctive nightlife. The rooftop of the opera house is a well-liked location for social gatherings and nighttime strolls since it offers breathtaking views of the city.

These are but a few illustrations of Oslo's nighttime possibilities. The nightlife culture in the city is vibrant and continually evolving, with new venues and events appearing all the time. To learn about the newest hotspots and activities during your visit, it's always a good idea to check local listings and ask residents for advice.

3.2 Bergen

On Norway's southwest coast is the lovely city of Bergen. It is renowned for its breathtaking natural beauty, magnificent historical buildings, and thriving cultural environment. An overview of Bergen's top attractions is provided below:

3.2.1 Bergen's top Attractions

Bryggen Hanseatic Wharf is the well-known waterfront district of Bergen and is a UNESCO World Heritage Site. It includes vibrant wooden structures that originally housed the Hanseatic League's offices and warehouses. It has stores, galleries, and restaurants today and is a well-liked tourist destination.

Take the Flibanen funicular up Mount Flyen or climb there to see sweeping views of Bergen. It's a wonderful location for picnics, outdoor activities, and taking in the breathtaking scenery.

One of Norway's oldest and best-preserved strongholds, Bergenhus Fortress is situated close to the harbor. It consists of the Rosenkrantz Tower, Hkon's Hall, and numerous other old structures. The history and architecture of the city can be discovered through guided excursions.

Fresh fish, regional vegetables, and souvenirs can be purchased at the lively Fish Market (Fisketorget), which is situated in the center of Bergen. It's a terrific spot to sample traditional fish meals from Norway.

Troldhaugen: Previously the residence of eminent composer Edvard Grieg, Troldhaugen is now a museum honoring his life and contributions. Take a tour of the composer's cottage, attend concerts, and take a stroll through the lovely grounds.

In the family-friendly Bergen Aquarium, you can see a wide range of marine animals, such as penguins, seals, fish, and sea lions. Visitors can take part in feeding sessions and discover more about Norway's maritime ecosystems.

Schtstuene and the Hanseatic Museum: The Hanseatic Museum offers a look into the daily activities and trade of the Hanseatic merchants in Bergen throughout the Middle Ages. The Schtstuene, which is next to the museum, provides details on the social and professional life of the Hanseatic League.

Bergen Art Museum (KODE): In Bergen, KODE is a grouping of various art museums and galleries. It holds a substantial collection of artwork from Norway and other countries, including pictures, sculptures, and decorative items.

Gamlehaugen: The royal palace in Bergen, Gamlehaugen is a stunning mansion situated on the beaches of the Nordsvannet lake and surrounded by gardens. It offers guided tours and is accessible to the general public at various times of the year.
One of the oldest churches in Bergen is St. Mary's Church (Mariakirken), which dates to the 12th

century. Both the architecture and the stained glass windows are stunning.

These are only a few of Bergen's numerous attractions. The city is a must-visit location in Norway due to its attractiveness, extensive history, and breathtaking natural surroundings.

2.2 The best Restaurants and Bars

Bergen is renowned for its thriving culinary scene, which offers a variety of dining options to accommodate all preferences and tastes. Some of Bergen's top restaurants and bars are listed below:
Bryggen Tracteursted is a historic eatery that provides traditional Norwegian cuisine. It is situated in the well-known Bryggen neighborhood. With meals like fish soup, reindeer, and cured salmon, it creates a warm and rural ambiance.

Seafood Restaurant Enhjrningen: This establishment is renowned for its tasty and fresh seafood meals. Enhjrningen, a quaint wooden establishment close to the Fish Market, serves delicacies including lobster, smoked salmon, and Bergen fish soup.

Lysverket is a well-known restaurant that fuses art and cuisine, and it is located in KODE 4. It provides a diverse menu with dishes that pay homage to the region's culinary tradition and are inspired by seasonal and local ingredients.

Pingvinen: A well-liked neighborhood bar serving comfort food from Norway. Meatballs, lamb stew, and fish cakes are just a few of the items on the menu. It's a wonderful location to take in the warm ambiance and savor substantial Norwegian cooking.

Colonialen Litteraturhuset: Colonialen is a café and restaurant that emphasizes fine ingredients and culinary artistry. It is housed in the Litteraturhuset (House of Literature). From sandwiches to salads to more complex meals, it offers a variety of foods.

Spisekroken: This quaint, small-scale eatery is renowned for its elegant, seasonally-inspired fare. With a focus on regional products, it offers a tasting menu highlighting the finest of Norwegian and foreign flavors.

Bryggeloftet & Stuene is a well-known eatery that provides traditional Norwegian food. It is housed in a historic building on Bryggen. It provides food including lamb shank, cod, and fish cakes in a warm, traditional setting.

Bare Vestland is a cutting-edge restaurant that emphasizes showcasing the flavors of Western Norway. It is situated in the heart of the city. It provides a varied menu with dishes produced with ingredients found locally.

Hoggorm Pizza is a must-visit location for pizza enthusiasts. It offers wood-fired pizzas made in the Neapolitan style with premium ingredients and inventive toppings. The experience is enhanced by the welcoming setting and helpful staff.

Vinbaren p Flien is a wine bar with sweeping views over Bergen that is situated on Mount Flyen. It provides a variety of wines, artisan brews, and light fare, making it the ideal place to unwind and take in the view.

These are only a few suggestions; Bergen offers a wide variety of dining establishments. Bergen boasts cuisine to suit every taste, whether it's traditional

Norwegian fare, seafood specialties, or cosmopolitan dishes.

3.2.3 Shopping

Bergen has a range of shopping options, including both conventional markets and contemporary shops. The following are some of Bergen's top shopping

districts and locations:
Bryggen: In addition to being a UNESCO World Heritage site, the old Bryggen neighborhood is an excellent place to shop. You can discover a variety of stores offering traditional Norwegian goods here, including apparel, jewelry, souvenirs, and crafts. Discover unique objects that represent Bergen's cultural past by exploring the little alleyways.

One of Bergen's main shopping streets is Strandgaten, which is situated in the heart of the city. It has a variety of department stores, specialist retailers, and high-street brands. Along this busy boulevard, you may buy clothes, accessories, electronics, books, and more.

Galleriet is a shopping center with a variety of stores and boutiques that is close to Torgallmenningen, the town's main square. It sells electronics, home goods, cosmetics, and clothing brands. In the event that you need a break from shopping, the mall also contains cafes and restaurants.

Another shopping center in the center of the city is called Bergen Storsenter. It has a range of stores, including specialty stores, jewelry stores, and clothing businesses. The mall is renowned for its broad range of designer brands and practical placement.

Kjttbasaren is a historic market building close to the Fish Market. It's a terrific location to discover and buy for regional foods, such as farm-fresh meat, cheese, and baked goods. There are speciality stores that sell spices, oils, and other foodstuffs.

Lagunen Storsenter: A sizable shopping complex near Bergen is located at Lagunen Storsenter if you're prepared to leave the city center a little. There are several different stores there, including ones for fashion, accessories, home goods, electronics, and more.

vre Ole Bulls Plass: Boutiques and specialist stores line this beautiful plaza. You may buy designer clothing, handmade jewelry, one-of-a-kind fashion items, and home décor with a Scandinavian flair here. It's a terrific place to look around and find regional designers.

Skostredet is a bustling street in Bergen that is well-known for its small boutiques and oddball stores. Local designers, vintage apparel, art galleries, and specialty stores can all be found there. Bergen's alternative and artistic side can be experienced by strolling around Skostredet.

Christmas Market at Bergen Handelsgymnasium: During the holiday season, Bergen Handelsgymnasium's courtyard is transformed into a delightful Christmas market. You can peruse the stalls here for handcrafted items, holiday decorations, regional specialties, and presents.

Farmers' Markets: Bergen is home to a number of excellent farmers' markets. Fresh fruit, regional foods, handmade cheeses, baked pastries, and other things are available at the Mathallen Market and Bergen Green Market. These markets are great for discovering Bergen's culinary offerings and promoting regional farmers.

These shopping alternatives in Bergen offer a variety of possibilities, from conventional handicrafts to contemporary clothing. Enjoy scouring the numerous markets, streets, and shopping centers for one-of-a-kind finds and mementos to take back home.

3.2.4 Entertainment

A wide range of bars, pubs, clubs, and live music venues can be found in Bergen, which has a vibrant nightlife. The following are some of Bergen's top nightlife destinations:

Nightclubs in Bryggen: The Bryggen region is home to a number of nightclubs that offer a variety of musical styles and ambiances. Dance the night away to pop, hip-hop, or electronic music at places like Garage, Hulen, and Kvarteret.

Hndverkeren: A well-liked bar with a lively environment and a large selection of craft beers, it is situated in the heart of the city. It's a terrific place to meet people, take in live music, and sample regional breweries.

Legal: A hip bar and club with a stylish atmosphere and a variety of music genres, Legal is located close to the Fish Market. It frequently offers themed parties and events and features both regional and international DJs.

Pingvinen: In addition to being a famous restaurant, Pingvinen is also well-known for its vibrant nightlife. This welcoming bar offers a selection of beers and drinks and is well-known for its welcoming ambiance and live music events.

No Stress is a laid-back bar with a laid-back ambiance that is renowned for its vast drink menu. It's a fantastic location for having a drink, mingling, and listening to live music or DJs spinning a variety of genres.

Ole Bull Scene is a well-known concert location that features a range of acts, such as live music, comedic performances, and theatrical productions. To find out what's going on while you're there, look over their schedule.

Ricks: Ricks is a popular nightclub with a younger clientele that features a variety of music genres, including pop, dance, and hip-hop. There are numerous dance floors, bars, and a buzzing environment there.

Hulen: Known for its alternative and indie music scene, Hulen is an underground music venue housed in a former bomb shelter. It offers unique and individualized experiences by hosting live performances by regional and international musicians.

Garage Bergen is a well-known club that specializes in electronic music, such as techno, house, and EDM. Its dynamic atmosphere and mix of local and international DJs make it a favorite among fans of electronic music.

These are just a few examples of Bergen's diverse range of nightlife alternatives. To accommodate various tastes and preferences, the city provides a wide variety of locations and events. For the newest hotspots and events during your visit, like with any nightlife scene, it's always a good idea to check local listings and ask locals for ideas.

3 2.5 Recommendations for Hotels in Bergen

There are numerous possibilities for lodging in Bergen to match various spending limits and preferences. Here are some suggestions for accommodations in Bergen:

The Radisson Blu Royal Hotel is a contemporary hotel with stylishly decorated rooms that is conveniently located in the heart of the city. It has facilities like a fitness center, a restaurant, and a bar and offers easy access to popular destinations.

Scandic rnen: This modern hotel, which is close to the train station, has spacious rooms and a variety of services. A rooftop patio, a restaurant, a fitness facility, and panoramic views of Bergen are available to visitors.

The exquisite rooms at Bergen Brs Hotel, which is located in a historic structure on the well-known Torgallmenningen Square, have opulent amenities. It is close to several attractions and offers a restaurant, a bar, and a fitness facility.

This boutique hotel, the Thon Hotel Rosenkrantz, is situated in the center of Bergen, near to Bryggen and other important landmarks. It offers chic accommodations with contemporary conveniences, free breakfast, and a comfortable lounge area.

Hotel Oleana: Located in the picturesque Nordnes area, this hotel provides cozy, creatively decorated rooms. It is conveniently situated between the waterfront and the city's core and includes a rooftop patio with expansive views.

The historic Bryggen neighborhood's Magic Hotel Korskirken has modern accommodations with distinctive décor. It is renowned for its convenient location, chic furnishings, and helpful personnel.
On the ocean, the waterfront Clarion Hotel Admiral offers cozy accommodations with breathtaking harbor views. It has a rooftop terrace, a bar, and a restaurant. The hotel is ideally situated close to Bryggen and other sights.

One of Bergen's oldest hotels, the Augustin Hotel was built in 1909 and combines classic charm with contemporary conveniences. It has a comfortable bar and restaurant and is conveniently situated close to the Fish Market and the Bryggen neighborhood.

Bergen Harbour Hotel: Situated in a charming old building on the busy Strandgaten street, Bergen Harbour Hotel provides welcoming and chic accommodations. Numerous attractions are close by and it has a friendly environment.

The Bergen YMCA Hostel offers inexpensive lodging with few amenities for those on a tight budget. It is conveniently situated close to the train station and provides both private rooms and dorm-style rooms.

These are but a few suggestions; Bergen offers a large selection of lodging choices, including hotels, boutique hotels, guesthouses, and hostels. To ensure your preferred choice, it is important to make reservations in advance, especially during the busiest travel times.

3.3 Tromso

An energetic city called Troms may be found in northern Norway, above the Arctic Circle. It is renowned for its breathtaking natural beauty, the captivating Northern Lights, and a variety of outdoor activities. Here is a description of Troms:

The largest city in Northern Norway is Troms, which is frequently referred to as the "Gateway to the Arctic." On the island of Tromsya, it is surrounded by stunning fjords, mountains, and a wide variety of species. With a blend of attractive wooden homes and modern architecture, the city has a rich cultural and historical legacy.

3.3.1 Major Sights:

One of the most well-known landmarks of Troms is the majestic cathedral. It is the only wooden cathedral in Norway and has a remarkable architectural style.

The Arctic Cathedral, sometimes referred to as Tromsdalen Church, is a stunning example of contemporary architecture across the Troms Bridge. It is well-known for both its stunning stained glass windows and unique triangular design.

The rich cultural and ecological history of the area is on display in the Troms University Museum. Archaeology, Sami culture, animals, and the Northern Lights are among the topics covered in its exhibitions.

Polaria: This educational museum and aquarium offers information on the marine life, climate change, and Arctic environment. Visitors can watch seals being fed and discover Arctic research.
Take a beautiful ride on the cable car to the summit of Mount Storsteinen with the Fjellheisen. Awe-inspiring panoramic views of Troms and the surroundings will be your reward from there.

The Troms Museum, a Northern Norway art museum, displays a variety of works of art, historical exhibits, and artifacts from the area and its past.

Visit the stunning botanical garden in Troms, which is home to a variety of plant species, including Arctic plants, wildflowers, and herbs.
Learn about the history of polar exploration and the expeditions that left from Troms at the Polar Museum. The museum features memorabilia and

narratives about illustrious explorers like Roald Amundsen.

3.3.2 The best Restaurants and Bars:

From cosmopolitan cuisines to traditional Norwegian fare, Troms provides a variety of dining options. Following are some suggestions for dining and drinking in Troms:

Emma's Drommekjokken: A quaint eatery with a reputation for its delectable and inventive Norwegian cuisine that emphasizes fresh, in-season ingredients.

Bardus Bistro: This restaurant serves a variety of cuisine, including fresh seafood, steaks, and vegetarian options, that are both Norwegian and foreign in origin. It boasts a lively environment and a large wine variety.

A seafood restaurant by the harbor, Fiskekompaniet is renowned for its delicious and fresh fish meals. Take pleasure in a selection of seafood, shellfish, and traditional Norwegian dishes.

Riso Mat & Kaffebar serves food that is both organic and regionally produced. Additionally to delicious baked pastries and speciality coffees, they provide a selection of vegetarian and vegan options.

Skarven: A well-known eatery on the seaside, Skarven provides traditional Norwegian fare like reindeer, salmon, and other local favorites.

Troms Mathallen is a food court with a number of vendors serving a variety of regional and international fare, including fish, hamburgers, Asian cuisine, and more.

The oldest bar in Troms, Lhallen has a welcoming ambiance and a large assortment of domestic and foreign brews. It's a terrific spot to meet locals and sample various beers.

Hildr Gastro Bar: This eatery combines international and Nordic flavors.

3.3.3 Shopping

There are many possibilities for shopping in Troms, ranging from hip chic boutiques to traditional Norwegian handicrafts. The following are some suggestions for shopping in Troms:

Just outside of the city center is a sizable shopping area called Jekta Storsenter, which has a variety of shops selling clothing, accessories, electronics, household products, and other items. It serves as a one-stop shop for all of your shopping requirements. Nerstranda Shopping Center is a well-known mall with a selection of stores, clothing boutiques, and restaurants located in the center of Troms. It is renowned for its handy location and cutting-edge design.

Troms Sentrum: The city's core is surrounded by quaint streets that feature a variety of stores, boutiques, and galleries. Discover one-of-a-kind apparel boutiques, gift shops, and regional artists by exploring Storgata, the main street, and its side alleyways.

The Polaria complex's gift shop, which is called Polaria, sells a variety of mementos, outfits, and things with Arctic themes. It's a fantastic location to find one-of-a-kind souvenirs of your trip to Troms.

Troms Handelshus is a large department store in the heart of the city that sells a range of items, such as apparel, accessories, home goods, and cosmetics. It is renowned for both its broad assortment and affordable costs.

Galleri Nord: Galleri Nord is a place to go if you enjoy art and crafts. It displays the creations of regional artists and artisans, including ceramics, jewelry, paintings, and sculptures.

Troms Kunstforening: This gallery and store features works of contemporary art made by local and foreign artists. Limited-edition pieces, prints, and original artwork are available.

In Troms Lapland, you may find a variety of traditional Sami products and souvenirs, including reindeer hides, Sami jewelry, traditional clothes, and artwork with Sami influences.

Arctic Gift Shop: This store, which sells gifts and mementos with Arctic themes, is located next to the

Arctic Cathedral. It offers a range of apparel, accessories, postcards, and home goods.

Farmers' Market: Don't miss the Farmers' Market hosted in the city center if you visit Troms in the summer. Locally grown cuisine, fresh fruits and veggies, flowers, and handcrafted goods are all available here.

Always double-check the store's opening times because they may change, especially on weekends and during holidays. Additionally, bear in mind that Norway's costs can be higher than those in other nations, so it's a good idea to budget appropriately.

3.3.4 Entertainment

In particular during the winter months when the city enjoys arctic nights, Tromso is renowned for its thriving nightlife. In Tromso, some of the well-known bars and clubs are:

lhallen: For anyone interested in experiencing the local culture, a visit to this old tavern, often known as the "Beer Hall," is a must. It offers a selection of drinks and appetizers in a welcoming, traditional setting.

Locals and visitors to the area enjoy the rock-themed pub and nightclub known as Bl Rock Café. Throughout the week, it holds DJ nights and live music events.

Driving: This cultural venue is well-known for its theatrical productions, live music events, and other cultural activities. Additionally, there is a bar and nightclub there that provides refreshments.

The tiny Rorbua Pub, which is close to the harbor, offers a selection of beers and regional Norwegian cuisine. Throughout the week, it also holds other events, including live music.

The fashionable Bastard Bar offers a wide selection of cocktails, beers, and nibbles. It hosts DJ nights and other events and has a relaxed environment.

Fruene: This cocktail establishment is renowned for its distinctive beverages and welcoming ambiance. Additionally, it offers a selection of small meals and snacks.

Café 3B: Both locals and tourists frequent this café/bar. It offers a selection of drinks and nibbles in a welcoming, laid-back setting.

Tromso provides a wide variety of nightlife alternatives, ranging from conventional pubs to cutting-edge bars and nightclubs.

3.3.5 Suitable Accommodation

There are numerous possibilities for lodging in Tromso to match various spending limits and preferences. Here are some suggestions about where to stay in Troms:

The trendy rooms at the conveniently located Clarion Hotel The Edge have lovely views of the city or the lake. It has attractions including a rooftop terrace, a fitness facility, and a restaurant right there.

The Radisson Blu Hotel Troms is a welcoming lodging option with easy access to the city's attractions. It is located near the port. It offers expansive views of the nearby mountains and fjords and has a restaurant, a bar, and a fitness facility.

The Scandic Ishavshotel offers cozy rooms with contemporary conveniences and is close to the Polar Museum. Popular sights are close by, and it offers a restaurant and bar with expansive views of the port.

Clarion Collection Hotel Aurora: This charming boutique hotel provides comfortable accommodations with a welcoming ambiance. It offers a free breakfast, a buffet for afternoon snacks, and dinner. A sauna and exercise facilities are also available to visitors.

The Thon Hotel Troms is a handy hotel with pleasant accommodations that is located in the heart of the city. It has a bar, a fitness facility, and a restaurant. The hotel is close to restaurants, shops, and tourist destinations.

Scandic Grand Troms: This conveniently placed hotel provides cozy accommodations and quick access to the city's top sights. It has a bar, a fitness facility, and a restaurant. In addition, the hotel provides bicycle rentals for city exploration.

Troms Lodge & Camping: This lodge and camping site offers a variety of lodging alternatives, including cabins and camping spaces, for those who want a more natural setting. It is close to the water and provides breathtaking views of the landscape.

If you want to visit the Svalbard archipelago, stay at the Radisson Blu Polar Hotel Spitsbergen, which is in Longyearbyen and has cozy accommodations and modern conveniences. The location is excellent for Arctic expeditions.

These are just a few suggestions; Troms offers a variety of lodging choices, including hotels, guesthouses, and vacation rentals. To ensure your preferred choice, it is important to make reservations in advance, especially during the busiest travel times.

3.4 Trondheim

Norway's third-largest city is Trondheim, which is situated in the middle of the country. Trondheim, which is renowned for its extensive history, beautiful architecture, and thriving cultural scene, provides a blend of traditional charm and contemporary attractions. An outline of Trondheim is shown below:

The Viking King Olav Tryggvason established Trondheim in 997 AD, and it functioned as Norway's capital until the 13th century. With a population of almost 200,000, it is a vibrant city today. The majestic Nidaros Cathedral, the largest medieval structure in Scandinavia, is one of Trondheim's most well-known examples of its rich medieval past.

Bakklandet, the city's historic core, is a charming district with vibrant wooden buildings, constrained cobblestone streets, and welcoming cafes. With a lovely ambiance and distinctive stores, it is a well-liked tourism destination for both locals and visitors.

Several renowned universities, notably the esteemed Norwegian University of Science and Technology (NTNU), are located in Trondheim. This adds to the city's vibrant and young atmosphere, which is complemented by a thriving student community and a vast variety of cultural and educational activities.

Trondheim has a thriving cultural scene in addition to historical and architectural landmarks. Numerous celebrations are held in the city throughout the year, such as the St. Olav Festival, which honors

Trondheim's patron saint, and the Trondheim International Chamber Music Festival, which features performances of top-notch classical music.

The closeness of stunning landscapes to Trondheim will appeal to nature enthusiasts. There are chances for boating, fishing, and other water sports in the adjacent Trondheim Fjord. Hiking, skiing, and other outdoor activities are available in the nearby mountains and forests.

The culinary scene in Trondheim is vibrant and fascinating, with a variety of eateries offering both local specialties and delicacies from around the world. The seafood in the city is well-known, especially the fresh salmon and cod.

Overall, Trondheim is a city that skillfully combines natural beauty, culture, and history. Trondheim has much to offer any visitor, whether they want to explore its historical monuments, take in its cultural offerings, or simply spend time outdoors.

3.4.1 Popular Destinations

Visitors can enjoy a variety of sites in Trondheim. The following are a few of Trondheim's most popular sights:

Nidaros Cathedral is a spectacular Gothic cathedral and the most recognizable structure in Trondheim. It is often referred to as Nidarosdomen. It serves as St. Olav's ultimate resting place, who is also Norway's patron saint. Visitors can take in religious ceremonies, view a display of royal regalia, and admire the beautiful architecture.

The Archbishop's Palace is a medieval palace that now serves as a museum, and it is close to Nidaros Cathedral. Through its exhibitions and artifacts, it provides insight into the history and culture of the Trondheim archbishopric.

Old Town Bridge, also known as Gamle Bybro, is a famous pedestrian bridge that spans the Nidelva River. The attractive Bakklandet neighborhood, famed for its vibrant wooden buildings, cafes, and shops, is connected to the city center by this bridge.

The bridge provides expansive views of the river and the surrounding area.

Rockheim is an interactive museum devoted to the history of rock music in Norway. The country's music scene can be studied through exhibitions, concert video, and educational materials available to visitors.

Kristiansten Fortress: Kristiansten Fortress, perched atop a hill overlooking Trondheim, provides sweeping views of the city and its surroundings. It is a fortification from the 17th century that has been carefully preserved and offers insight into Trondheim's military past.

Just outside of the city center lies the open-air Sverresborg Trndelag Folk Museum, which features examples of traditional Norwegian architecture and way of life. It has more than 80 historic structures, including a stave church, a farm, and a workshop.

Tyholt Tower is a communications tower with an observation deck where you can get a bird's-eye view of Trondheim. The views of the city and its surroundings are breathtaking.

Take a boat ride to the little island of Munkholmen in the Trondheim Fjord. It was once a monastery and then turned into a prison. Today, tourists can take a picnic, unwind on the beach, or explore the ancient remains.

The Trondheim Science Center (Vitensenteret) is a great place for families and science enthusiasts to learn about a variety of scientific concepts through interactive displays, workshops, and educational activities.

These are but a few of Trondheim's numerous attractions. The wide variety of attractions in Trondheim are sure to enthrall and fascinate visitors, regardless of their interests in history, architecture, nature, or culture.

3.4.2 The Best Restaurants and Bars

There are many restaurants, cafes, and pubs in Trondheim to accommodate a wide range of preferences. Some of the top places to eat and drink in Trondheim are listed below:

The intimate and rustic environment of this restaurant, Baklandet Skydsstation, is found in the lovely Bakklandet neighborhood. It delivers regionally sourced, modernized versions of traditional Norwegian cuisine. Try the reindeer stew or the renowned cinnamon cakes from Baklandet.

Credo: Sustainable and locally sourced foods are a priority at this Michelin-starred establishment. Seasonal menu changes feature creative meals with classic Norwegian flavors. It provides a distinctive dining experience in a fashionable atmosphere.

To Rom og Kjkken: This eatery is well-known for its imaginative and tasty meals produced with regional products. The restaurant boasts a warm, welcoming ambiance with a menu that combines inspirations from Norway and other countries.
Mathallen is a food hall with a variety of food stalls and restaurants that is situated in Solsiden, a neighborhood near the water. It serves a wide variety of foods, including sushi, tapas, burgers, and desserts. It's a terrific place to sample various cuisines in a relaxed atmosphere.

Fagn: A second Trondheim restaurant with a Michelin star, Fagn offers a unique dining experience with creative cuisine made with regional products. The restaurant offers a classy and cozy dining environment, and the food has been carefully chosen.

Den Gode Nabo: This bustling bar and eatery provides a welcoming ambiance and a large selection of beers on tap. It offers traditional pub fare like burgers, fish & chips, and filling sandwiches. Both locals and tourists like visiting it.
Located in the center of Trondheim, Cafe 3B is a well-liked hangout for locals. It offers a selection of beverages, such as coffee, beer, and cocktails. It's the perfect place for a light lunch or a drink with friends.

Ramp Pub & Spiseri: This bar and restaurant is located in the heart of the city and is renowned for its welcoming atmosphere and extensive beer menu. The menu features classic pub fare like burgers, fish meals, and vegetarian selections.

Grünerlkka Brygghus: This local tavern and microbrewery serves a variety of locally brewed craft beers. It's a terrific location to try out regional beers and take in the laid-back environment. Along with the beers, pub-style food is also offered.

The Bakklandet neighborhood is home to the modest cocktail bar Bare Blbaer. It specializes on handcrafted drinks using premium ingredients. The pub features a cozy, laid-back atmosphere that is ideal for an evening drink.

These are but a few suggestions; there are many more fantastic eating and drinking establishments in Trondheim that you might discover. No matter what your taste in food is—traditional Norwegian fare, tastes from around the world, or hip cocktail bars—Trondheim has it all.

3.4.3 Shopping

With a mixture of contemporary retail centers, quaint boutiques, and speciality businesses, Trondheim offers a varied shopping experience. Following are some of Trondheim's well-known shopping areas and outlets:

Trondheim's major shopping strip is Nordre Gate, which is situated in the heart of the city. It is lined with many different shops, including department stores, gift shops, and fashion boutiques. Both domestic and foreign brands can be found here.

Solsiden is a contemporary shopping and leisure complex that is located by the water. It has a variety of stores, eateries, cafes, and a movie theater. Fashion, accessories, home goods, and other items are available.

Trondheim Torg: In the center of the city lies a shopping center called Trondheim Torg. It has a number of shops that sell things like clothing, accessories, gadgets, and housewares. A supermarket and food court are also located in the center.

Bakklandet: Bakklandet is a lovely neighborhood with a variety of quaint boutiques and speciality stores. It is well-known for its picturesque wooden cottages and cobblestone streets. You may find distinctive goods here, including artisanal goods, locally produced art, and handmade crafts.

Byhaven: Byhaven is a cutting-edge shopping mall near to the city's core. There are many shops there, including ones for fashion, beauty, technology, and home furnishings. There are numerous food options at the center.

If you appreciate secondhand shopping, Fretex Secondhand is a store you should check out. It is a well-known thrift shop where you can find used furniture, clothing, and other stuff. The store's earnings go to charitable organizations.

Markets and Flea Markets: Throughout the year, Trondheim hosts a number of markets and flea markets that provide a distinctive shopping experience. Watch for occasions like the Torvet Market, where you may buy local goods, fresh fruit, and handicrafts.

Trondheim is home to a number of antique stores where you can browse and discover old treasures. These stores frequently provide a wide variety of goods, such as furniture, jewelry, works of art, and collectibles.

Nidarosdomens Gullsmedverksted: This jewelry shop, which sells handcrafted silver and gold jewelry influenced by Norse customs, is close to Nidaros Cathedral. Unique items with elaborate designs are available.

Local Food Shops: You may buy regional specialties including cheese, cured meats, chocolates, and traditional Norwegian goods at speciality food stores in Trondheim. These stores are fantastic for food lovers and people looking for culinary mementos.

Keep in mind to double-check each store's opening times because they may change. In order to satisfy a variety of tastes and preferences, Trondheim offers a variety of shopping possibilities, whether you're seeking for clothing, souvenirs, regional goods, or one-of-a-kind items.

3.4.4 Entertainment

There are many bars, pubs, clubs, and live music venues in Trondheim, making for a vibrant nightlife scene. In Trondheim, these are some of the hotspots for nightlife:

Olav Tryggvasonsgate: This city center street is lined with various bars and taverns, making it the core of Trondheim's nightlife. Numerous places can be found that offer a range of settings and libations.

Work-Work is an innovative blend of a coworking space, bar, and gaming lounge that is situated in the Bakklandet neighborhood. With board games, vintage gaming consoles, and a variety of craft brews, it offers a laid-back atmosphere.

Familie: This chill pub and club is well-known for its diverse playlist of indie, rock, and electronic music. It is well-liked by both locals and tourists since it exudes an air of coziness and intimacy.

Fru Hagen: A hip pub serving a variety of craft brews, cocktails, and wines, Fru Hagen is located close to the Nidaros Cathedral. It regularly presents live music events and has a lively environment.

Café 3B: During the day, Café 3B is a well-liked place for coffee, but at night, it changes into a buzzing bar. It provides a comfortable and laid-back ambiance, making it a fantastic location to unwind with a drink and mingle.

Café 3BRETT: Located next to Café 3B, 3BRETT is a board game café where you and your friends can relax with a drink while playing a variety of board games. It's a lively place to hang out with friends.
The Villa is a well-known nightclub in Trondheim with various dance floors and a varied music

selection that includes EDM, hip-hop, and pop. Local and foreign DJs and performers perform there.

Ramp Pub & Spiseri: This city center bar features a laid-back ambiance, a large beer variety, and sporadic live music events. It's a fantastic location for having drinks and hanging out with friends.

Café 3R is a hip cocktail bar with a reputation for having an inventive drink menu. It is situated in the Solsiden neighborhood. It provides a chic and contemporary atmosphere, making it a well-liked option for cocktails and a night out.

Dokkhuset is a concert hall where a range of live musical acts take place, such as jazz, classical, and world music. In Trondheim, it's an excellent spot to experience live music.

These are only a few alternatives for Trondheim's nightlife. Trondheim's nightlife culture has something for everyone, whether you're searching for a chill pub, an energetic club, or live music. The city offers a variety of places catering to diverse preferences.

3.4.5 Suitable Accommodation

There are a variety of lodging alternatives in Trondheim to accommodate all tastes and price ranges. Here are some suggestions for lodging in Trondheim:

Britannia Hotel: The opulent five-star Britannia Hotel is situated in the center of Trondheim and is renowned for its chic interior design and first-rate service. It provides numerous eating options, a spa, and accommodations that are roomy and luxuriously furnished.

The Scandic Nidelven is a contemporary and chic hotel with lovely city views along the Nidelva River. It has spacious accommodations, a gym, a riverside restaurant, and a rooftop patio.

The Radisson Blu Royal Garden Hotel offers convenient access to the city's heart, cozy accommodations, a fitness facility, and a restaurant. It provides quick access to places of interest such the Trondheim Torg shopping center and Nidaros Cathedral.

By the port in Trondheim, the Clarion Hotel offers modern rooms with views of the water or the city. It has a restaurant on-site, a fitness center, and a rooftop bar. The city's attractions may be easily explored thanks to the location's centrality.

Travelers may easily access the Comfort Hotel Park because of its ideal location close to Trondheim Central Station. It has cozy accommodations, a health club, and a hip lobby bar.

Thon Hotel Nidaros: Located in the heart of the city, the Thon Hotel Nidaros features cozy accommodations, a free breakfast buffet, and a fitness facility. Popular sights like Nidaros Cathedral and Trondheim Torg can be reached on foot.

P-Hotels Brattra: This inexpensive hotel is close to Trondheim Central Station and has simple yet cozy rooms. It offers simple access to transit and is close to sights like Solsiden and the Nidaros Cathedral by foot.

Trondheim Vandrerhjem: Trondheim Vandrerhjem is a wonderful choice if you're seeking for inexpensive lodging. Both individual rooms and dormitory-style rooms are affordably priced. A common kitchen and lounge are available in the hostel, encouraging interaction among guests.

Trondheim offers a wide range of Airbnb alternatives, from individual rooms to complete apartments or homes. For individuals seeking a more tailored and at-home experience, this can be a terrific option.
Think about things like location, amenities, and your budget when making hotel reservations in Trondheim. To guarantee availability, it is important to book reservations well in advance, especially during the busiest travel times.

3.5 Stavanger:

The bustling city of Stavanger is situated on Norway's southwest coast. It is the fourth-largest city in the nation and renowned for its thriving oil sector, stunning natural surroundings, and rich cultural legacy. An overview of Stavanger is shown below:

History: The Viking Age is where Stavanger's lengthy history began. It was a significant commerce centre that eventually developed into a significant fishing industry hub. Due to its closeness to offshore oil reserves in the North Sea, it is now known as Norway's oil capital.

Architecture: The buildings in Stavanger combine old and new styles. Gamle Stavanger, a picturesque old town, is home to 18th-century timber buildings that have been meticulously kept. It is a well-liked tourist destination and one of the largest remaining wooden home villages in Europe.

Natural Grace: Beautiful natural scenery surrounds Stavanger. The stunning Lysefjord, which is close by, is known for its high cliffs and pristine seas. The Preikestolen (Pulpit Rock) and Kjerag, which offer superb hiking and picturesque vistas, are two of its most well-known attractions.

A variety of museums and cultural attractions can be found in Stavanger. With roots in the 12th century, the Stavanger Cathedral is both a famous landmark and a significant location in Norwegian ecclesiastical history. Insights into art, history, and the oil business can be found at other museums like the Stavanger Art Museum, Norwegian Petroleum Museum, and Stavanger Maritime Museum.

Food and Dining: There are many restaurants and cafes in Stavanger, which boasts a thriving culinary scene. Many regional eateries serve fresh fish and seafood meals because the city is well-known for its seafood. The largest culinary festival in Scandinavia, the annual Gladmat Festival, which takes place in Stavanger each year, features both regional and international cuisine.

Outdoor Activities: Stavanger has a wide range of outdoor activities due to its close proximity to fjords, mountains, and beaches. Popular activities for both locals and tourists include hiking, kayaking, fishing, and boat tours. The area serves as a starting point for trips to the picturesque surroundings of Ryfylke and the well-known Trolltunga hiking path.
Festivals and Events: Throughout the year, Stavanger holds a number of festivals and events. Along with the Gladmat Festival, it also honors the Stavanger Jazz Festival, MaiJazz Festival, and NuArt Festival, which presents modern and contemporary urban art on the streets.

transit: There are flights to major European cities from Stavanger's international airport, which is part of a well-connected transit network. Additionally, the city has a robust network of public transit that includes buses and ferries, making it simple to explore the surroundings.

The combination of natural beauty, cultural attractions, and a vibrant city life in Stavanger is exceptional. Every visitor may find something to enjoy in Stavanger, whether they want to explore historical places, go on outdoor activities, or indulge in gastronomic treats.

3.5.1 Popular Destinations

There are a number of prominent attractions in Stavanger that highlight the history, natural beauty, and cultural legacy of the area. Some of the must-see sights in Stavanger are listed below:

Explore the charming alleyways of Gamle Stavanger, the city's historic area, in Gamle Stavanger (Old Stavanger). It has magnificent and nostalgic wooden residences from the 18th and 19th centuries that are superbly preserved.

Visit the Stavanger Cathedral, usually referred to as the Stavanger domkirke, in Stavanger, Norway. It was built in the 12th century, making it Norway's oldest cathedral. The cathedral's interior features stunning stained glass windows in addition to its remarkable architecture.

Visit the Norwegian Petroleum Museum to learn more about the influence and intriguing history of Norway's oil industry. Understanding the exploration, production, and technological breakthroughs in the oil industry is possible thanks to interactive exhibitions, models, and multimedia displays.

Take a hike to the well-known Pulpit Rock, also known as Preikestolen, by visiting it. This cliff's flat top rises 604 meters above Lysefjord, providing breathtaking panoramic views. It takes about 4 to 5 hours to trek to Pulpit Rock.

Lysefjord: To see the spectacular splendor of the Lysefjord, take a boat excursion or a fjord cruise. The fjord is distinguished by its sheer cliffs, emerald seas, and picturesque waterfalls. Nature's treasures like Pulpit Rock and Kjerag can be seen up close on the voyage.

Stavanger marine Museum: The Stavanger Maritime Museum is a great place to learn about the city's seafaring heritage and marine history. The exhibitions provide visitors a glimpse into the city's maritime legacy through historical antiques, ship models, and interactive displays.

Visit the Norwegian Canning Museum to learn more about the past of the area's once-vibrant canning industry. The museum is housed in a former cannery and has displays that show how cans are made, what it was like to work there, and how it affected Stavanger.

For sweeping views of Stavanger, climb the Valberg Tower (Valbergtrnet). This medieval tower gives visitors a look into the city's past and a vantage point from which to take in the surroundings.

Stavanger Art Museum: The Stavanger Art Museum, which has a sizable collection of Norwegian artwork from the 19th and 20th centuries, is a must-see for art fans. Famous Norwegian artists including Edvard Munch and Harald Sohlberg have pieces in the museum.

Enjoy a tranquil day at the lovely sand beach at Sola Strand, which is close to Stavanger. This beautiful beach is ideal for swimming, sunbathing, and leisurely stroll along the shoreline.

These top Stavanger attractions include a variety of historical, cultural, and outdoor adventures that perfectly encapsulate the spirit of the city and its environs.

3.5.2 The Best Restaurants and Bars

With a large selection of eateries, cafes, and pubs serving both regional and international food, Stavanger has a thriving culinary scene. Some of the top places to eat and drink in Stavanger are listed below:

You may purchase fresh fish and seafood in the bustling fish market known as Fisketorget, which is close to the waterfront. Fish soup, grilled fish, and shrimp are just a few of the mouthwatering seafood delicacies available at the many seafood stalls and restaurants.

Popular restaurant Renaa Matbaren is renowned for its creative and excellent Norwegian food. A variety of traditional and contemporary dishes made with ingredients acquired locally are offered on the menu.

Ostehuset is a beautiful cafe and bakery that serves a range of delectable meals. They offer a variety of cheeses, freshly baked bread, pastries, sandwiches, and salads. It's a terrific spot for a relaxed breakfast, lunch, or cup of coffee in the afternoon.

Tango Bar & Kjkken is a chic eatery that offers fusion dishes of Norwegian and international cuisine. The restaurant has a warm and lively ambiance, and the menu includes meals produced using seasonal ingredients.

Renaa: Renaa is a fine-dining establishment with a Michelin star. The menu features inventive and exquisitely presented dishes made with an emphasis on organic and locally sourced ingredients.

Café 1900: This quaint cafe is well-known for its handcrafted pastries, cakes, and light fare. It's a terrific spot to indulge in delectable sweet delicacies while sipping coffee or tea.

Blgen & Moi: Situated on a stunning waterfront, Blgen & Moi is a well-known restaurant. The eatery is renowned for its exquisite and inventive culinary presentations and for its varied menu that combines cuisines from Norway and other countries.

Cardinal Pub: If you enjoy beer, you must go to Cardinal Pub. It offers a wide variety of artisan brews from Norway and other countries. The pub boasts a welcoming and laid-back ambiance that makes it ideal for sharing a pint with friends.

Hekkan Burger: For burger aficionados, Hekkan Burger is a well-known restaurant. They provide a selection of gourmet burgers, including vegan and vegetarian choices, all created with premium ingredients.

Gnu Bar: This hip cocktail bar has a lively vibe. They specialize in inventive drinks that are carefully made. It's a fantastic location for relaxing and savoring a well-made beverage.

These are only a few of the numerous dining establishments in Stavanger. Stavanger has a variety of dining options to suit any taste, whether you're looking for traditional Norwegian fare, delicacies from around the world, or informal restaurants.

3.5.3 Shopping

Stavanger has a variety of shopping alternatives, including boutique shops, neighborhood markets, and contemporary malls. Some of the top places to shop in Stavanger are listed below:

Arkaden Stavanger is a contemporary retail complex with a variety of stores, including clothing, accessories, electronics, and home products. It is situated in the heart of the city. Both international brands and Norwegian stores can be found there.

Stervg is a lovely street in the heart of Stavanger noted for its speciality shops, galleries, and boutique shops. Unique clothing, regional handicrafts, works of art, and design products are all available here.

Klverhuset is a shopping area located close to the waterfront. There are a variety of high-end fashion labels, lifestyle shops, and eateries there. A panoramic view of the waterfront and the neighborhood is also provided by the center.

In close proximity to Stavanger Cathedral lies the Stavanger Domkirke Antikk- og Bruktmarked. It offers a huge selection of furniture, jewelry, ceramics, and other treasures, making it a treasure trove for antique enthusiasts.

Lagrdsveien is a well-known shopping street featuring a mix of national chains, neighborhood boutiques, and specialized shops. Along this busy boulevard, you may buy clothes, shoes, accessories, and more.

Kvadrat Shopping Center: Situated west of Stavanger, Kvadrat is one of Norway's biggest shopping centers. With more than 170 stores, it offers a wide range of food options, technology, fashion, and home design.

You can browse and buy a variety of foods supplied locally at Mathallen Stavanger, a food market located in Stavanger, Norway. It offers locally produced specialized goods, fresh fruit, cheese, meats, and baked goodies.

Stavanger Torget: The major market area in the heart of the city is where you can find stalls selling locally made goods, fresh produce, flowers, and fruits. It's a fantastic location for picking up fresh ingredients and taking in the vibe of the neighborhood.

Lkkeveien: Lkkeveien is a well-liked street recognized for its chic boutiques, specialized shops, and retailers. Unique fashion goods, Scandinavian design products, and items for home décor are all available here.

Strmsteinsgrden: Strmsteinsgrden is a historic structure that is home to a number of stores and shops. It has a variety of specialist shops, home products, fashion, and accessory retailers.
These Stavanger shopping areas offer a selection of options for fashion, design, regional goods, and more. Every type of consumer will find something in Stavanger, whether they are looking for well-known brands, unusual goods, or a taste of regional cuisine.

3.5.4 Entertainment

With a selection of bars, clubs, and entertainment venues, Stavanger has a thriving and energetic nighttime culture. The following are some of the top locations in Stavanger for experiencing the nightlife: Checkpoint Charlie is a well-liked nightclub in Stavanger that is renowned for its upbeat ambiance and dance music. It offers a variety of musical styles and frequently showcases live DJs and acts.

Cardinal Pub: Cardinal Pub is a comfortable location to unwind and have a few drinks in addition to being a terrific place for beer fans. It has a wide variety of craft beers from all around the world, a relaxed ambiance, and welcoming service.

'Bker og Brst' is a distinctive pub that combines a bar and a bookstore. It offers a welcoming and laid-back atmosphere where you may unwind with a variety of refreshments while perusing the literature.

Hexagon Bar is a chic cocktail lounge renowned for its inventive and expertly made cocktails. The bar boasts a chic atmosphere that makes it a fantastic spot to spend time with friends or on a date.

Checkers Sports Bar: For sports fans, Checkers Sports Bar is the place to go. It has a lively environment, numerous TVs showing live sports events, a large selection of drinks, and pub fare.

Alf & Werner: In the center of Stavanger, there is a well-known pub and restaurant called Alf & Werner. It has a varied menu that includes many different drinks and cocktails. The bar is an excellent place for entertainment because it frequently has live music performances.

Hall Toll: Housed in a heritage structure, Hall Toll is a hip bar and eatery. It offers a large variety of drinks, live music, and a warm, relaxing ambiance. Both locals and tourists like visiting it.

Sting Nere: Sting Nere is a live music venue where both national and international artists frequently perform and hold concerts. Rock, jazz, and blues are just a few of the many musical genres that are played there.

Tou Scene: An historic brewery now serves as the home of Tou Scene, a cultural hub. It holds a variety of events, such as parties, concerts, and exhibits. It is a distinctive location that draws a wide variety of people and provides a lively nightlife experience.
The Irishman Pub is a quaint, real Irish pub that is situated in Stavanger. There is live music, a large selection of Irish beers, and a traditional pub atmosphere.

These are just a few examples of Stavanger's many nightlife offerings. There is something for everyone to enjoy once the sun goes down thanks to the city's broad selection of venues that appeal to all tastes and interests.

3.5.5 Suitable Accommodation

Here are some suggestions for lodging in Stavanger: The Radisson Blu Atlantic Hotel is a contemporary property with outstanding amenities and a prime location close to Stavanger's top attractions.

Clarion Hotel Stavanger: This waterfront hotel offers chic accommodations, a rooftop terrace with panoramic views, and a full-service restaurant.
The Scandic Stavanger City offers cozy accommodations, a fitness facility, and a restaurant right in the middle of the action. Popular sights and shopping districts may both be reached on foot from the property.

Comfort Hotel Square: This hip hotel is renowned for its sleek interiors, cozy accommodations, and lively environment. It is close to the city's core and provides quick access to dining establishments and nightlife.

Thon Hotel Maritim: This hotel, which is located close to the port, provides guests with comfortable and well-appointed rooms, a restaurant on the premises, and a handy location close to Stavanger's top attractions.

In addition to providing cozy accommodations, a fitness facility, and an on-site restaurant serving international cuisine, the Radisson Blu Royal Hotel in Stavanger enjoys a prime location close to the city's historic district.

The Scandic Stavanger Park is a hotel with roomy accommodations, a fitness facility, and a restaurant close to the city's core. Popular attractions and parks are accessible by foot.

In the center of Stavanger, the quaint Best Western Havly Hotell provides welcoming accommodations, a welcoming lounge area, and a free breakfast. It is close to restaurants, stores, and tourist sites.

Myhregaarden Hotel: This boutique hotel, housed in a historic structure, has individually furnished rooms with contemporary conveniences. It offers a distinctive and fashionable lodging experience and is close to the city core.

For guests looking for self-catering lodgings, City Housing provides completely equipped apartments in a convenient location at Kirkebakken 8. The furnished flats offer a feeling of home away from home.

Just a few of the preferred lodging options in Stavanger are included here. The city provides a variety of options to fit various spending limits and interests, providing a relaxing and pleasurable stay while you are there.

3.6 The Fjords

3.6.1 Geirangerfjord

One of Norway's most well-known and stunning fjords is Geirangerfjord. It is situated in western Norway's Mre og Romsdal county's Sunnmre region. The Geirangerfjord is well known for its breathtaking natural beauty, including its deep blue waters, magnificent waterfalls, and steep, snow-capped mountains that rise sharply from the fjord.

Here are some of Geirangerfjord's main characteristics and draws:

Scenic Beauty: Geirangerfjord, a UNESCO World Heritage Site, is frequently referred to as the "Jewel of the Norwegian Fjords." The fjord is about 15 kilometers (9 miles) long and is bordered by towering cliffs and thick vegetation, which creates a beautiful panorama.

Waterfalls: The fjord is ornamented by a number of stunning waterfalls, such as the Seven Sisters and Bridal Veil waterfalls, which are both well-known. These waterfalls stream down the jagged mountain slopes, making for an amazing spectacle.
The Geiranger Skywalk, which gives panoramic views of the fjord and the surrounding landscapes, is located atop the mountain Dalsnibba. It is one of Norway's highest vistas, rising 1,500 meters (4,900 feet) above the surrounding terrain.

Fjord cruises: One well-liked method of discovering Geirangerfjord is by taking a fjord cruise. The cruises offer a chance to go across the serene waters of the fjord, observe the majestic cliffs, and come up close to the waterfalls. A lot of cruises also provide enlightening narration on the geology and history of the region.

Outdoor activities such as hiking are available in Geirangerfjord, allowing tourists to explore the fjord and its environs on foot. The routes range from short strolls to strenuous hikes that provide beautiful vistas. Popular outdoor pursuits in the region include kayaking, fishing, and wildlife observation.

Geiranger: Located at the head of the fjord, the little community of Geiranger provides as a base for tourists exploring the region. It provides lodging alternatives, dining establishments, cafes, and retail stores. The fjord's natural splendor and the village's pleasant and tranquil environment combine to provide a wonderful setting.

The greatest time to visit Geirangerfjord is in the summer when the weather is pleasant and the days are long. The fjord can become congested during the summer months because it is a well-liked tourist destination. Consider traveling during the shoulder seasons of spring or autumn to avoid the crowds.

Geirangerfjord guarantees a remarkable experience of Norway's natural treasures, whether you decide to join a fjord cruise, stroll along the paths, or simply gaze the stunning view.

3.6.2 Hardangerfjord

Another beautiful fjord in Norway is called Hardangerfjord, and it can be found in the counties of Hordaland and Vestland on the country's southwest coast. With a length of about 179 kilometers (111 miles) from the Atlantic to the town of Odda, it is the second-longest fjord in Norway.
Here are some of the main characteristics and draws of Hardangerfjord:

Hardangerfjord is noted for its breathtakingly beautiful scenery, which includes deep blue waters, high mountains, lush green valleys, and tumbling waterfalls. Fruit orchards, woodlands, and lovely villages are just a few of the stunning surroundings that surround the fjord.

Hardangerfjord is well known for its fruit orchards, especially apple orchards. Fruit farming thrives here thanks to the area's rich soil and pleasant temperature. The orchards bloom in the spring with lovely flowers, creating a lively and colorful sight.
Waterfalls: From the nearby mountains, various waterfalls drop down into the fjord. The 182-meter (597-foot) high Vringsfossen is one of the most

well-known waterfalls in the region. It is a well-liked attraction and provides a breathtaking spectacle.

Trolltunga: Trolltunga is a well-known hiking location in the Hardanger region, despite not being situated right on the fjord. The unusual rock structure, which protrudes horizontally over the mountainside and provides breathtaking panoramic views of the fjord and the surrounding area, is situated on a plateau.

Folgefonna National Park is a spotless region famous for its glacier, Folgefonna, and the surrounding sceneries. It is located close to the Hardangerfjord. The park provides a variety of outdoor pursuits, such as skiing, glacier treks, and wildlife spotting.

Hardangerfjord is home to traditional Norwegian communities, old churches, and museums that highlight the history and customs of the area, making it rich in cultural heritage. Visit the Hardanger Folk Museum in Utne to discover more about the people and culture there.

Outdoor Activities: There are many chances for outdoor activities like hiking, fishing, kayaking, and cycling in and around the fjord. The well-known Queen Sonja Panoramic Hiking Route is one of many hiking routes that offer breathtaking views.

Norheimsund: Situated on the Hardangerfjord's northern shore, Norheimsund is a lovely settlement. In addition to a waterfront promenade and cultural attractions like the Hardanger Maritime Museum, it has a lovely port.

The Hardangerfjord is a year-round vacation spot, and each season has its unique allure. The best times to take advantage of the fruit orchards in bloom and engage in outdoor activities are in the spring and summer. Autumn shows the vibrant foliage, and winter offers chances to participate in winter activities and take in the tranquil fjord views.

The Hardangerfjord offers a mesmerizing and awe-inspiring glimpse into Norway's natural beauties and cultural legacy, whether you want to explore the fjord by enjoying a picturesque drive along its banks, setting out on a fjord cruise, or setting out into the nearby mountains.

3.6.3 Sognefjord

The longest and deepest fjord in Norway is called Sognefjord, and it is situated on the country's western coast in the county of Vestland. From the shore near the town of Solund to the settlement of Skjolden at the deepest portion of the fjord, it is about 205 kilometers (127 miles) long. The spectacular majesty, unspoiled scenery, and lovely settlements of Sognefjord are well known.

Here are some of Sognefjord's main characteristics and draws:
Sognefjord is renowned for its breathtaking natural beauty, which includes snow-capped mountains, rocky outcrops, tumbling waterfalls, and calm blue waters. The fjord is surrounded by verdant landscapes, charming settlements, and lush valleys, creating an enthralling and dramatic scene.

Nryfjord: A section of Sognefjord recognized for its stunning and narrow fjord landscape, Nryfjord is a UNESCO World Heritage Site. With its soaring mountain sides and spectacular vistas, it is regarded as one of the most beautiful fjords in the entire world. Fjord cruises and kayak tours are two ways to see Nyfjord.

Flm: The Sognefjord shoreline is home to the thriving tourist attraction of Flm. It has stunning scenery, including one of the steepest trains in the world, the Flm Railway, which gives breathtaking views of the surrounding mountains and waterfalls.
The biggest glacier in all of continental Europe, Jostedalsbreen, is found in the Jostedalsbreen National Park, which is close to Sognefjord. The park offers guided excursions, glacier walks, and stunning views of the icy surroundings.

Outdoor Recreation: Sognefjord and the area around it offer a wealth of chances for outdoor pursuits like hiking, riding, fishing, and kayaking. In addition to providing panoramic views of the fjord and its surroundings, including the well-known Aurlandsdalen Valley, there are various clearly defined hiking trails.
Historic stave churches, or wooden churches constructed in the Middle Ages, can be found at Sognefjord. These distinctive buildings serve as historical and cultural landmarks and shed light on Norway's illustrious past.

Balestrand: A delightful community recognized for its picturesque environment and old structures, Balestrand is situated on the northern coast of Sognefjord. It has beautiful fjord views, cultural attractions, and outdoor recreation opportunities.

Every season in Sognefjord has its own allure, making it a popular visit all year long. Winter offers possibilities for winter sports and enjoying the tranquil fjord environment blanketed in snow, while the summer months are popular for boating around the fjord or participating in outdoor activities.

Exploring Sognefjord enables you to take in Norway's breathtaking natural beauty and the serenity of the fjord's surrounds. Sognefjord guarantees a remarkable and alluring experience whether you opt to join a fjord cruise, explore the picturesque trails, or simply take in the breathtaking views.

3.6.4 Nordfjord

Located in western Norway's Vestland county, Nordfjord is a charming fjord. The distance from the Jostedalsbreen National Park to the open sea at Stad is around 106 kilometers (66 miles). Nordfjord is renowned for its breathtaking natural surroundings, imposing mountains, and quaint coastal settlements. Here are some of Nordfjord's main characteristics and draws:

Scenic Beauty: The spectacular natural beauty of Nordfjord is highlighted by its deep blue waters, soaring mountains, and verdant valleys. The fjord is surrounded by breathtaking nature, including glaciers, waterfalls, and undulating hills, which makes for an enthralling and varied panorama.
A portion of the Jostedalsbreen National Park, which is well-known for its spectacular glaciers, notably the well-known Briksdal Glacier, is located in Nordfjord. Visitors can go on guided excursions or hike to views to see the amazing ice creations and appreciate nature's strength.

The Loen Skylift is a cable vehicle that transports people from the fjord's bottom to Mount Hoven's summit. You may get sweeping views of Nordfjord, the surrounding mountains, and the adjacent towns from the peak. The Loen Skylift offers a singular and exhilarating view of the fjord.

Coastal Villages: The picturesque coastal communities that dot Nordfjord provide a look into the local culture and traditional Norwegian architecture. There are possibilities to learn about the fishing business, visit historical monuments, and consume fresh seafood in places like Mly and Selje.

Hiking and Outdoor Activities: For nature lovers, Nordfjord provides a variety of outdoor activities. There are many hiking trails with accommodations for all skill levels, offering chances to explore the region around the fjord, including the mountains and valleys. Popular outdoor pursuits in the region include fishing, kayaking, and wildlife observation.
Olden: At the eastern extremity of Nordfjord, in the village of Olden, cruise ships frequently dock. It provides as a point of entry to natural treasures including the stunning Lake Olden and the Briksdal Glacier. Visitors can stroll through the village, browse the stores, or go on fjord cruises.

Nordfjord is a year-round vacation spot, and each season has its own special allure. While the winter months offer opportunity for skiing and taking in the tranquility of snowy landscapes, the summer months offer comfortable weather for outdoor pursuits and exploration.

Nordfjord offers a spectacular and immersive experience of Norway's natural wonders and coastal charm, whether you decide to go on a fjord cruise, hike the trails, or just relax and take in the peace and quiet of the surroundings.

3.7 Northern Norway

3.7.1 Lofoten Islands

The Lofoten Islands are a group of islands in Norway's north, above the Arctic Circle. The Lofoten Islands are frequently cited as one of Norway's most gorgeous locations due to their spectacular scenery, craggy mountains, immaculate beaches, and traditional fishing settlements. The Lofoten Islands are described in great detail below:

Authentic Beauty The breathtaking natural splendor of the Lofoten Islands is what makes them unique. There are many islands in the archipelago, including Austvgya, Vestvgya, Flakstadya, and Moskenesya. Magnificent mountains, fjords, deep valleys, and white sand beaches dominate the scene. A wonderfully breathtaking backdrop is created by the union of the dramatic coastline, pure waters, and picturesque panoramas.

Outdoor Recreation: The Lofoten Islands provide a wealth of activities for hikers and outdoor lovers. Visitors may explore the various landscapes and take in breath-taking views from elevated vantage points thanks to the abundance of hiking paths that are suitable for hikers of all levels of experience. The hikes Reinebringen, Tindstinden, and Mannen are all well-liked. Fishing, kayaking, birdwatching, and cycling are further outdoor pursuits.

Fishing towns: The lovely fishing towns that dot the islands provide visitors a glimpse of the traditional Norwegian way of life. Reine,, Nusfjord, and Henningsvaer are just a few of the towns famous for their lively docks, beautiful wooden buildings, and functioning fishing boats. Visitors can enjoy fresh seafood, take in the local culture, and visit art galleries.

Wildlife and birdwatching: A wide variety of wildlife can be found on the Lofoten Islands. Along the coast, there's a chance you'll see seagulls, otters, reindeer, and seals. Birdwatchers love to visit the islands to see the puffins, sea eagles, and guillemots that make their nests in the cliffs and rocky outcrops. The Lofoten Islands experience the midnight sun phenomena throughout the summer months because of their location above the Arctic Circle. The sun doesn't set from late May until mid-July, giving you 24 hours of daylight. This rare natural phenomena enables extensive outdoor exploration and recreation. In contrast, the islands provide a good site for viewing the hypnotic Northern Lights (Aurora Borealis) moving across the night sky during the winter.

Fishing and seafaring traditions are a significant part of the Lofoten Islands' rich cultural heritage. The Stockfish Museum in offers insights into the traditional stockfish production, which has been a mainstay industry in Lofoten for generations, while the Lofotr Viking Museum in Borg highlights the region's Viking heritage.

Photography and art: Photographers and painters from all over the world have been drawn to the gorgeous vistas of the Lofoten Islands. The mix of imposing mountains, glistening fjords, and charming settlements provides countless options for taking beautiful pictures and producing works of art.

Local cuisine: The Lofoten Islands are famed for their delectable fish dishes. High-quality stockfish, dried cod, and other delectable fresh seafood products are produced in the islands. Indulge in seafood feasts at neighborhood restaurants and sample regional specialties like lutefisk and bacalao (lye-cured dried fish).

The Lofoten Islands provide a variety of lodging choices, including hotels, guesthouses, and cabins, giving tourists an opportunity to fully experience the distinctive mood and natural surroundings of the island.
The Lofoten Islands offer everything you're looking for, whether you're looking for tranquility, breathtaking scenery, or cultural events.

3.7.2 North Cape

North Cape, commonly referred to as Nordkapp, is a well-known landmark situated in the northernmost region of European Union territory. It is located on the Norwegian island of Magerya in the county of

Finnmark. The North Cape is renowned for its breathtaking cliffs, expansive vistas of the Arctic Ocean, and significance as the northernmost point on the European Continent. Here is a thorough description of North Cape:

Geographical Importance: North Cape is an important geographic landmark since it is located at a latitude of 71°10'21" north. It is frequently referred to as the "Top of Europe" and is thought to be the northernmost point on the European Continent that is reachable. Visitors can get a sense of being at the edge of the world by standing at the cliff's edge.

Scenic Beauty: The steep cliffs that stand roughly 307 meters (1,007 feet) above the Arctic Ocean in the area surrounding North Cape are what give the area its rocky coastline environment. Even more so at the midnight sun or when the Northern Lights are lighting up the sky, the views from the cape are just magnificent. The desolate but breathtakingly gorgeous surroundings add to the attractiveness of this famous location.

Facilities & Visitor Center: The North Cape Visitor Center is a cutting-edge building that serves visitors' needs. It provides a variety of attractions, such as a panoramic cinema, exhibitions, dining options, coffee shops, and retail stores. Through multimedia presentations and interactive exhibits, the center offers perspectives on the history, culture, and environment of the area.

Polar Nights and the Midnight Sun: North Cape is renowned for its extraordinary natural phenomena. From mid-May until late-July in the summer, the area enjoys the midnight sun. This results in 24 hours of daylight because the sun does not set below the horizon. Seeing the sun at midnight is a fascinating sight. On the other hand, North Cape experiences polar nights during the winter, when the sun never rises over the horizon and there is a period of nonstop darkness.

Sami Culture: The North Cape area has a long history with the indigenous Sami people. The opportunity exists for visitors to learn about the Sami people's traditional way of life, including reindeer herding and Sami crafts. Those desiring to fully experience the culture can partake in activities such as touring a Sami camp, learning about Sami folklore, and dining on local cuisine.

species: A variety of species can be seen in and around North Cape. Visitors may have the opportunity to see marine mammals like seals and whales as well as seabirds like puffins and sea eagles. The Arctic off-coastal seas are well-known for their diverse species and offer fantastic chances for wildlife observation.

Activities and Exploration: In addition to taking in the breathtaking views from the cliff, visitors to North Cape can take part in a number of other activities. Popular activities include hiking, fishing, birdwatching, and exploring the local shore and fishing communities. A boat journey to explore the North Cape from the water also provides a distinctive viewpoint and an opportunity to spot seabird colonies and other marine life.

North Cape is accessible all year round, and every season has its own allure and natural beauty. North Cape offers a unique experience and a sense of being on the edge of the earth, whether you are drawn to the midnight sun, the Northern Lights, or simply the lonely and breathtaking surroundings.

3.7.3 Senja Island

A hidden treasure in northern Norway, Senja Island is renowned for its beautiful scenery, untamed mountains, picturesque fjords, and quaint fishing communities. Senja, sometimes referred to as "Norway in miniature," has a wide variety of outdoor sports and natural attractions. Here is a thorough description of Senja Island:

Natural Beauty Senja Island is the ideal destination for those who enjoy the outdoors and a spectacular, diversified scenery. The island's beautiful mountains, deep fjords, white sandy beaches, and lush woods are its defining features. Stunning visuals are produced by the contrast between the rocky beach and the high Alps.

Senja is recognized for its breathtaking alpine beauty, which includes the recognizable Segla and Hesten peaks. These mountains offer fantastic hiking options, with routes appropriate for hikers of all experience levels. A photographer's dream, ascending to the summits provides panoramic vistas of the nearby fjords and coastal sceneries.

Senja Island is surrounded by a number of fjords, including the well-known Mefjord and Ersfjord.

These fjords offer breathtaking views of sheer cliffs that plunge into the pristine seas. Additionally, Senja has lovely sandy beaches, including Bvaer Beach and Tungeneset Beach, where guests can unwind, swim, or have a picnic.

Senja Island offers a great chance to see the captivating Northern Lights, often known as the Aurora Borealis. The island has ideal circumstances for seeing this natural occurrence in the winter because of its remote location and little light pollution. An memorable experience is created for visitors by the dancing lights in the dark skies.

Senja Island is home to a variety of wildlife and provides possibilities for birdwatchers and other wildlife enthusiasts. Reindeer, moose, sea eagles, seals, and otters are among the many creatures that call the island home. To see these wonderful species in their native habitat, tourists can go on wildlife safaris or explore the shoreline.

Senja Island is home to a number of lovely fishing communities that have managed to maintain their authentic charm. With their vibrant homes, bustling fishing ports, and seafood eateries, villages like Gryllefjord, Hamn i Senja, and Husy provide a look into the island's fishing tradition. Visitors can sample local cuisine, learn about the culture, and engage with the welcoming residents.

Senja Island offers a variety of outdoor activities to satisfy a variety of interests. In addition to hiking and wildlife viewing, tourists can go fishing, kayaking, cycling, and on boat excursions to explore the nearby fjords and coastal regions. The island's varied topography offers countless options for exploration and adventure.

Midnight Sun: Senja encounters the phenomena of the midnight sun in the summertime. Every day, the sun is still visible beyond the horizon, extending the time that may be spent outdoors and letting tourists take in the special atmosphere of the midnight sun.

Hotels, guesthouses, cabins, and camping sites are available as lodging alternatives on Senja Island, giving guests the chance to experience the island's natural beauty and the friendly friendliness of the residents.

Senja Island is a hidden gem that provides a mesmerizing fusion of outdoor adventures, natural beauty, and cultural experiences. Senja is guaranteed to create a lasting impact, whether you're looking for breathtaking scenery, close encounters with wildlife, or quiet tranquillity.

Activities in Norway

4.1.1 Hiking:

With its extensive wilderness, breathtaking scenery, and well-maintained paths, Norway provides a wealth of hiking opportunities. Here are a few well-liked hiking spots:

Trolltunga is one of Norway's most well-known treks, and it is situated in the Hordaland county. The 22-kilometer hike offers difficult but rewarding views of the fjords and the famous Trolltunga rock formation.

Preikestolen (Pulpit Rock) is a well-known hike that leads to a flat rock platform with stunning views of Lysefjord. It is located close to Stavanger. The four-kilometer track is manageable for hikers of all experience levels and is very flat.

Besseggen Ridge: The Besseggen Ridge walk in Jotunheimen National Park offers breathtaking views of Lake Gjende and Lake Bessvatnet. It is a difficult 14-kilometer hike that calls for the right hiking equipment and experience.

The Romsdal region's Romsdalseggen Ridge route offers sweeping views of the mountains, valleys, and fjords nearby. Although the 10-kilometer climb is difficult, it rewards hikers with stunning vistas.

The "Home of the Giants," Jotunheimen National Park, offers a variety of hiking opportunities, from day hikes to multi-day expeditions. The park is renowned for its majestic alpine vistas, glaciers, and towering peaks.

4.1.2 Skiing and snowboarding:

With so many resorts and backcountry regions to discover, Norway is a skiing and snowboarding enthusiast's dream. Here are a few famous places:

Hemsedal is one of Norway's biggest ski resorts, and it is situated in the Buskerud county. It provides a wide range of slopes for skiers of all abilities, contemporary amenities, and a buzzing après-ski scene.

The biggest ski resort in Norway is called Trysil, and it is located in the Hedmark county. There are several different slopes, terrain parks, and family-friendly amenities there.

Lofoten Islands: In northern Norway, the Lofoten Islands provide an exceptional skiing opportunity with stunning Arctic Ocean vistas. There are fantastic off-piste skiing options in these mountains.

Rldal: Situated in the county of Hordaland, Rldal is well-known for receiving a lot of snowfall, making it a popular spot for powder lovers. It has a combination of steep hills and wilderness terrain.

4.1.3 Kayaking and Canoeing

Norway is a great place to go kayaking and canoeing because of its extensive coastline, fjords, and lakes. Here are a few suggestions for places to go:

Geirangerfjord: You may experience the breathtaking fjord and its gushing waterfalls from a different vantage point by kayaking in the UNESCO-listed Geirangerfjord.

Lofoten Islands: The Lofoten Islands are a fantastic place to go kayaking thanks to their rocky shoreline and pristine waters. A unique experience is paddling through fjords and past breathtaking peaks.

Telemark Canal: For a tranquil canoe trip, head to the Telemark Canal in southern Norway. From Skien to Dalen, the canal travels through lovely landscapes and fascinating locks.

4.1.4 Fishing:

Both in freshwater lakes and the sea, Norway is recognized for its exceptional fishing prospects. Here are a few well-known fishing spots:

Laksforsen: One of Norway's most well-known salmon rivers, Laksforsen is found in the county of Nordland. In this picturesque river, anglers can try their luck catching salmon and other freshwater fish.

Islands of Lofoten: The Lofoten Islands are a well-liked spot for both sport and leisure fishing. You can go fishing in the Norwegian Sea's deep waters here, where you might catch fish including cod, halibut, and sea trout.
The "King of the Fjords," Sognefjord, is not only a beautiful natural beauty but also a fantastic place to go fishing. Salmon, trout, and cod are among the many fish species that call the fjord home.

Rros is a medieval mining town that is encircled by lakes and rivers in Trndelag county. These crystal-clear waterways, which are renowned for having an abundance of trout, are perfect for fishing.

4.2 Cultural Events:

4.2.1 Galleries:

In Norway, there are several different museums that provide insights into the country's rich history, culture, and artistic heritage. Among the notable museums are:

The Viking Ship Museum in Oslo offers visitors a look into Norway's Viking past by displaying well-preserved Viking ships and relics.

The Norwegian Museum of Cultural History (Oslo) is an outdoor museum that displays traditional Norwegian structures and cultural relics from various parts of the country. It is located on the Bygdy Peninsula.

The National Museum of Art, Architecture, and Design in Oslo is home to a sizable collection of Norwegian works of art from many eras, including paintings, sculptures, and decorative arts.

The Munch Museum (Oslo): This museum in Oslo houses a sizeable collection of famous Norwegian painter Edvard Munch's paintings, sketches, and graphic works.

4.2.2 Art Galleries:

Norway has a thriving art scene, and there are several galleries that exhibit a wide variety of modern and traditional artwork. Several notable art galleries are:

The Astrup Fearnley Museum of Modern Art (Oslo): This contemporary art gallery is located in Oslo and features works by both Norwegian and foreign artists.

The Henie Onstad Kunstsenter (Baerum), a museum and art center outside of Oslo, features a collection of modern and contemporary art in addition to changing exhibitions and live events.

The Bergen Kunsthall (Bergen): This gallery in Bergen is one of Norway's most well-known locations for contemporary art, hosting exhibitions, occasions, and performances by local and foreign artists.

4.2.3 Architecture:

Norway has a blend of historic and contemporary buildings. Among the famous architectural landmarks are:

The Oslo Opera House (Oslo): This contemporary masterpiece is renowned for its eye-catching design and waterfront setting. Visitors are welcome to stroll through the interior of the structure and gaze out from its rooftop.

The Nidaros Cathedral (Trondheim): This Gothic cathedral in Trondheim is a work of art and a significant place of worship. It is the largest medieval structure in Scandinavia.

The Arctic church in Troms is a famous church that stands out for its striking location and panoramic views of the city and surrounding mountains. It has a recognizable triangle design.

4.2.4 Music and Festivals:

Norway has an active festival scene and a thriving music culture. One of Norway's largest music festivals, yeah Festival is held in Oslo and has a broad lineup of musicians from throughout the world and Norway, representing a variety of musical styles.

The Bergen International Festival (Bergen) is a yearly celebration of music, dance, theater, and visual arts that draws well-known performers from all over the world.

Troms hosts the Midnight Sun Marathon, which has live music performances throughout the course and a fun environment. It takes place on the summer solstice.

4.3 Nature and Wildlife

4.3.1 Whale Watching:

Whale watching is very possible in Norway's coastal areas. Several areas where people go whale watching are:
The northern Norwegian island of Andenes (Vesterlen) is renowned for having a diverse marine population that includes sperm whales and orcas.

There are boat cruises offered for whale-watching outings.
Several whale species, including humpback whales and orcas, frequent the waters near Troms. You may get a close-up look at these gorgeous animals on guided trips.

4.3.2 Aurora Borealis/Northern Light:

The Aurora Borealis, often known as the Northern Lights, is a stunning natural phenomenon that may be seen in some parts of Norway. The following information on seeing the Northern Lights:

Troms, in northern Norway, is regarded as one of the best locations in the nation to see the Northern Lights. The city provides a variety of excursions and guided trips made especially for seeing the Northern Lights. Your chances of seeing the mesmerizing displays of colors dancing across the night sky are increased by the fact that these tours frequently transport you to isolated areas with little light pollution.

The Lofoten Islands offer the perfect setting for witnessing the Northern Lights because to their pristine landscapes and bright skies. For a chance to see this natural phenomenon, you can go on guided tours or even go on your own to remote beaches or mountaintops.

Svalbard: Svalbard, which is in the Arctic, provides a rare chance to see the Northern Lights in a distant and uninhabited wilderness. Due to the harsh weather and safety concerns, it is advised to join guided tours or expeditions conducted by expert guides.

Finnmark: Known for its Arctic vistas and favorable viewing conditions for the Northern Lights, Finnmark is the northernmost region of Norway. Many Northern Lights tours and activities, including dog sledding and snowmobile safaris paired with Aurora hunting, are available in towns like Alta and Kirkenes.

It is advised to travel to Norway during late autumn and early spring when the nights are longer and darker to increase your chances of viewing the Northern Lights. Additionally, the likelihood of seeing this natural event is increased by clear sky, little light pollution, and great solar activity.

Keep in mind that the Northern Lights are a natural phenomenon that can happen at any time. As it may take several nights of observation to see a clear show, persistence and patience are essential. Additionally, it's critical to pack warm clothing and be ready for the cold, especially if you're traveling in the winter.

Please be aware that depending on numerous variables including weather and solar activity, the precise locations and accessibility of Northern Lights sightings can change. For the most recent advice and information on Northern Lights experiences, it is always advised to check with local tourism offices or tour companies.

Norway's Food and Drink

5.1 Norwegian Traditional Food

5.1.1 Fish and seafood

Because of Norway's location along the coast and number of fjords, seafood is an important feature of traditional Norwegian cuisine. Here are a few examples of popular seafood dishes:

Gravlaks is a classic Norwegian meal made of thinly sliced fresh salmon that has been cured with salt, sugar, and dill. It is frequently served with a mustard and dill sauce and flatbread or toast.

Fiskesuppe is a substantial fish soup cooked with a variety of fish, such as cod, salmon, or halibut, as well as vegetables, herbs, and occasionally cream. It's a popular dish, especially around the shore.

Rakfisk is a fermented fish dish that is often made from trout or char. For several months, the fish is salted and fermented, giving in a distinct and pungent flavor. It is frequently served with onions and sour cream on flatbread.

Sild: Sild, or pickled herring, is a traditional Norwegian dish. Pickled herring is commonly marinated in a sweet or savory marinade that includes spices, onions, and herbs. It is served with sour cream or mustard sauce as a topping on bread or crispbread.

Lutefisk is a classic Norwegian meal made with dried and rehydrated whitefish, most commonly cod or ling. It undergoes a one-of-a-kind preparation process that includes soaking in lye, which gives the fish a jelly-like texture. It is frequently accompanied by boiled potatoes, peas, bacon, and mustard.

Game and meat
Norwegian cuisine also features a wide range of meat and game dishes. Here are a few examples:
Pinnekjtt (dried and salted lamb ribs): Pinnekjtt is a classic Christmas dish. Steamed over birch branches, the ribs are served with boiled potatoes, mashed rutabaga, and a robust sauce.
Smalahove: Smalahove is a classic Norwegian meal that is popular during the Christmas season. It's made with a salted, smoked, and boiled sheep's head. Traditionally, the meal is served with potatoes and rutabaga.

Reindeer meat is a delicacy in Norway, especially in the northern regions. It is frequently served as steaks or stewed, and its rich flavor complements lingonberry sauce and other traditional accompaniments.

Dairy Goods

Norway is well-known for producing high-quality dairy products. Among the most popular dairy-based foods and products are:

Brunost: Brunost, commonly known as dark cheese, is a whey-based Norwegian cheese. It tastes slightly sweet and has a caramel-like flavor. It is frequently served with bread or crispbread.

Rmmegrt: Rmmegrt is a sour cream porridge cooked with sour cream, flour, and butter. It is usually served with a sprinkle of cinnamon and sugar, and it is sometimes eaten with cured meats.

Krumkake is a thin, crisp waffle-like cookie made from flour, butter, sugar, and cream batter. It is frequently shaped into a cone and served with whipped cream or ice cream.

These are only a few examples of traditional Norwegian cuisine, which emphasizes marine, meat, and dairy items. The culinary legacy of Norway is diverse, with each region having its own specialties and variations. Exploring local markets, restaurants, and festivals is a terrific opportunity to learn about Norway's unique flavors and dishes.

Meat Dishes

Norwegian cuisine is known for its wonderful meat dishes. Here are some well-known examples:

Kjttkaker are typical Norwegian meatballs cooked with ground beef or pig, onions, breadcrumbs, and spices. They're usually accompanied by creamy gravy, cooked potatoes, and lingonberry jam.

Frikl: Frikl is a traditional Norwegian dish made of slow-cooked lamb and cabbage. It is frequently regarded as Norway's national dish and is generally consumed throughout the autumn months. The meal is spiced with black peppercorns and cooked until the meat is soft and the flavors combine.

Raspeballer: Raspeballer, also known as klubb or komle, are boiled potato dumplings made from mashed and grated potatoes, flour, and salt. They are frequently accompanied by boiled or fried bacon, sausages, and lingonberry jam.

Plse: In Norwegian cuisine, plse refers to sausages of various sorts and flavors. Grillplse (grilled sausage), wienerplse (Vienna sausage), and medisterplse (spiced pork sausage) are some popular varieties. Plse is usually accompanied by mustard, ketchup, and toppings such as crispy onions.

Norwegian smoked and cured meats are well-known for their great quality. Popular options include fenalr (cured lamb leg), spekeskinke (cured ham), and spekeplse (dry sausage). These meats are frequently thinly sliced and served on bread or as part of charcuterie platters.

Rmmegrt med spekemat is a typical dish that consists of rmmegrt (sour cream porridge) served with a range of cured meats such as spekeskinke (cured ham), fenalr (cured lamb leg), and spekeplse (dry sausage). It is a filling and hearty dinner that is frequently served at special occasions.

These are only a few examples of Norwegian beef dishes. Norway's culinary traditions vary by area, and diverse delicacies can be found throughout the country. Exploring local markets, butcher shops, and traditional restaurants will allow you to sample a variety of tasty meat-based dishes in Norway.

Pastries and Desserts

Norwegian desserts and pastries come in a wide variety of flavors and textures. Here are some popular sweet foods to try:

Krumkake is a thin, crisp waffle-like cookie made from flour, butter, sugar, and cream batter. It is frequently folded into a cone and filled with whipped cream or other delicious ingredients.

Kvaefjordkake: Also known as the "queen of cakes," kvaefjordkake is a stacked sponge cake with a creamy custard filling. It is frequently topped with meringue and almonds, which makes it both tasty and artistically appealing.

Skillingsboller: Skillingsboller are cinnamon buns from Norway. They're normally produced with a yeast-based dough that's been filled with butter, sugar, and cinnamon before being baked till golden brown. Skillingsboller are typically served with a hot cup of coffee or tea.

Bltkake is a traditional Norwegian sponge cake covered with whipped cream and fresh berries. It's a popular treat for birthdays and other special events, and the berries used change depending on the season.

Multekrem: A traditional Norwegian dessert made with cloudberries, a native berry found in Norway's northern regions. To make a delectable and tart dessert, the berries are boiled and combined with sugar and whipped cream.

Riskrem is a rice pudding delicacy that is popular during the Christmas season. Cooked rice, sugar, vanilla, and whipped cream are used to make it. A hidden almond is hidden in the pudding, and whomever finds it wins a tiny prize.

Fyrstekake (traditional almond tart): Fyrstekake is a typical almond pastry with a thick and buttery almond filling. It is frequently topped with a powdered sugar-dusted lattice design constructed from finely sliced almonds.

Marzipan: A popular sweet delicacy prepared from ground almonds and sugar, marzipan is a popular sweet delight. It is frequently formed into various shapes, such as fruits or animals, and can be eaten as is or used to decorate cakes and pastries.

These cakes and pastries are only a taste of the sweet treats available in Norwegian cuisine. They can be found in bakeries, cafes, or even cooked at home using traditional family recipes. Norwegian sweets are a tasty way to end a meal or a pleasant treat to enjoy throughout the day.

5.2 Alcoholic Beverages

Norway has a wide variety of beverages to quench your thirst and compliment your culinary adventures. Here are some well-known Norwegian beverages:

Aquavit
Aquavit is a culturally significant traditional Norwegian spirit. It is made from grain or potatoes and seasoned with herbs and spices such as caraway, dill, and anise. Aquavit is frequently served as an aperitif or with traditional Norwegian cuisine.

Beer: Beer is popular in Norway, and the country has a thriving craft beer culture. Traditional lagers, ales, stouts, and sour beers are among the beer styles produced by Norwegian breweries. Ringnes, Mack, and Ngne are some well-known Norwegian beer brands.

Cider: Norway has a thriving cider sector, offering a variety of refreshing apple and fruit ciders. These ciders are available in a variety of flavors, ranging from basic apple to more inventive blends that include berries and other fruits.

Coffee: Norwegians take their coffee seriously, and it is an important part of their daily lives. Norway has one of the highest coffee consumption rates in the world. Norwegian coffee is normally served black or with a splash of milk. Aside from conventional coffee, fashionable coffee shops offer customized brews and techniques.

Fruit Juices: Norway is well-known for producing high-quality fruit juices, particularly apple and berry juices. These juices are created from fruits grown locally and are popular as a pleasant and natural drinking alternative.

Kvass: A classic fermented beverage produced from rye bread and water, kvass is a traditional fermented beverage. It has a slightly sour and tangy flavor and is occasionally sweetened or flavored with fruits and spices. Kvass is a one-of-a-kind, non-alcoholic beverage to sample in Norway.

Arctic Water: Norway is well-known for its clean and pure water sources, which include glacier and

Arctic water. Bottled water from these sources is accessible, and it tastes pleasant and clean.

These are only a few of the beverages available in Norway. Whether you prefer alcoholic or non-alcoholic beverages, Norway provides a wide selection to satisfy every taste. Remember to drink responsibly and enjoy the distinct flavors of Norway.

5.2.3 Coffee

Coffee has a special position in Norwegian culture, and Norwegians are well-known for their affinity for the beverage. Here are some of the most important elements of coffee in Norway:

Coffee Consumption: Norwegians are among the world's top coffee users per capita. Coffee is an essential component of their daily routine, and they frequently consume it throughout the day.

Brewing techniques: Most Norwegians prefer brewed coffee to other techniques. A popular method is drip brewing, which uses coffee machines or filter cones. French press (presskanne) and espresso-based beverages such as cappuccinos and lattes are also popular.

Norwegians frequently drink their coffee black (svart). Small cups of strong black coffee are commonly provided after meals or at social occasions. It should be drank gently and enjoyed.

Kokekaffe: Kokekaffe is a traditional Norwegian brewing method in which coffee grinds are boiled in a pot of water. This approach is frequently connected with outdoor activities such as camping or hiking, and it is a way to enjoy a rich and powerful cup of coffee in the great outdoors.

Coffee Breaks: The Norwegians have a cultural idea known as "kaffepause," which translates to "coffee break." It is a treasured custom in which individuals take a break from work or everyday duties to have a cup of coffee and chat with colleagues, friends, or family.

Coffee Quality: Norwegians place a premium on high-quality coffee. Many Norwegian households ground their coffee beans fresh before brewing to ensure that the flavor and aroma are excellent. Specialty coffee shops and micro-roasteries, which provide a diverse selection of artisanal and single-origin coffee beans, are also growing in popularity.

Coffee Culture: There are many coffee shops and cafes in Norwegian cities and towns. They offer warm and inviting areas for individuals to gather, work, or simply enjoy a cup of coffee. To accompany your coffee, Norwegian cafes frequently serve a range of pastries, sandwiches, and snacks.

When in Norway, have a cup of traditional black coffee or explore the contemporary speciality coffee scene to immerse yourself in the coffee culture. Norway has a rich coffee culture that is sure to satisfy any coffee enthusiast, whether you enjoy a traditional cup of drip coffee or a painstakingly constructed espresso-based beverage.

Norwegian shopping

6.1 Souvenirs and Presents

When it comes to souvenirs and presents in Norway, you'll discover a diverse selection that reflects the country's history, heritage, and natural beauty. Consider the following popular souvenirs and gift ideas:

Handicrafts: Norway is well-known for its rich handicraft culture. Hand-knit woolen sweaters (known as "norsk genser"), mittens, and socks are examples of products that are not only functional but also reflect traditional Norwegian patterns and designs. Popular wooden products include carved figurines, ornamental bowls, and culinary equipment.

Goods Inspired by the Vikings: Norway has a deep connection to its Viking heritage. Consider buying Viking-inspired things like jewelry with Norse symbols like Thor's hammer (Mjolnir) or the Vegvisir compass. Viking swords, shields, and helmet replicas are also available, making for distinctive and historically relevant gifts.

Norwegian Food goods: Purchase Norwegian food goods to bring a taste of Norway home with you. Brown cheese (brunost), cured salmon (gravlaks), cloudberries (multe), and traditional biscuits like krumkake and lefse are all available. These things make excellent gifts for foodies or pleasures for yourself.

Sami Crafts: The Sami people have their own culture and craftsmanship. Look for duodji (traditional Sami crafts) such as finely carved silver jewelry, reindeer leather accessories such as purses and wallets, and handwoven woolen items such as hats and mittens.

Art and Design: Norway has a strong art sector, with a wide range of artwork, prints, and designs capturing the country's beauty. Look for works that are influenced by landscapes, fjords, and wildlife. You can also visit contemporary art galleries and shops to find one-of-a-kind and trendy art items.

Trolls are legendary beings with strong roots in Norwegian tradition. Troll figurines, which are often fashioned of wood or pottery, are popular souvenirs. They come in a variety of sizes and styles, making them unique and whimsical gifts.

Norway has a rich literary past, and books by Norwegian authors are thoughtful gifts. Seek out works by Henrik Ibsen, Knut Hamsun, Sigrid Undset, and Jo Nesb. Books on Norwegian mythology, history, and nature are also available.

Consider shopping for souvenirs and gifts at local markets, specialist shops, and tourist centers in places such as Oslo, Bergen, and Troms. These establishments frequently offer a diverse range of unique and locally created products that embody the character of Norway.

6.2 Design and Fashion

Norway has a thriving fashion and design scene, noted for its distinct blend of modern style, Nordic aesthetics, and functional designs. When it comes to fashion and design shopping in Norway, there are numerous possibilities to fit a variety of tastes. Here are some crucial points to consider:

Norwegian Designers: Talented fashion designers from Norway develop innovative and sustainable apparel and accessories. Look for Moods of Norway, Holzweiler, Cathrine Hammel, and Norwegian Rain, among other well-known Norwegian fashion labels.

These labels provide high-quality clothing with a particular Norwegian flair.

Traditional Norwegian dress: Explore traditional dress components to embrace your Norwegian ancestry. Look for handcrafted woolen sweaters, cardigans, and accessories with traditional Norwegian patterns such as the classic "Selburose" pattern. Bunads, traditional Norwegian costumes used for special events, are also popular, but they are usually custom-made and more expensive.

Concept Stores & Boutiques: Discover a selected variety of local and worldwide fashion brands at concept stores and boutiques in key cities such as Oslo, Bergen, and Trondheim. These shops typically sell a mix of apparel, accessories, and home decor goods that combine current and Nordic design concepts.

Explore Scandinavian fashion labels that emphasize clean lines, simple designs, and utilitarian style in addition to Norwegian designers. Brands such as Filippa K, Acne Studios, COS, and Ganni provide a Scandinavian look that appeals to Norwegian fashion sensibilities.

Eco-Friendly and Sustainable Fashion: Norway places a high value on sustainability and environmentally friendly activities. Seek out fashion labels that stress ethical production, employ organic materials, or recycle items in their collections. Sustainable fashion stores and initiatives are becoming more popular, providing aware buyers with a variety of options.

Handmade & Artisanal Crafts: Norway is well-known for its artisanal crafts and handmade accessories, in addition to its fashion. Local markets, craft fairs, and independent stores are great places to find one-of-a-kind jewelry, leather products, purses, and accessories made by local artisans.

Interior Design & Homeware: Norway has a wide range of design stores and boutiques for anyone interested in interior design and homeware. Look for clean lines, natural materials, and Scandinavian design aesthetics in furniture, lighting, textiles, ceramics, and home decor products.
Consider visiting popular retail streets and places in Norway for fashion and design, such as Karl Johans gate in Oslo, Torgallmenningen in Bergen, and Nordre gate in Trondheim. Keep an eye out for

pop-up markets and events that feature rising designers and independent firms.

6.3 Outdoor Gear and Equipment

Norway is famous for its stunning natural beauty, and outdoor activities such as hiking, skiing, and camping are particularly popular. If you intend to participate in these activities, you will need the proper gear and equipment. Here are some of the greatest sites in Norway to buy outdoor clothing and equipment:

XXL Sport & Villmark: XXL Sport & Villmark is Norway's largest sports and outdoor retailer, with locations in numerous cities across the country. They have a large selection of gear and equipment for hiking, skiing, camping, and other outdoor activities, as well as sports such as football and cycling.
Fjellsport.no is an online retailer specializing in outdoor apparel and equipment. They sell hiking, skiing, and climbing equipment, as well as camping gear and clothes.

Norrna: Norrna is a popular Norwegian outdoor apparel and equipment brand both in Norway and overseas. They sell high-quality outdoor clothes and equipment for hiking, skiing, and other outdoor activities.

Bergans is another well-known Norwegian outdoor apparel and equipment company. They sell items for hiking, skiing, and other outdoor activities, as well as apparel for regular use.

Anton Sport: Anton Sport is a sports and outdoor retailer with locations across Norway. They provide a comprehensive choice of outdoor gear and equipment, as well as apparel and footwear for sports such as football and jogging.

6.4 Local Markets and Commercial districts

Exploring local markets and shopping districts is an excellent way to immerse yourself in the colorful ambiance of Norwegian cities and villages while discovering unique products and local crafts. Here are some of Norway's best local markets and retail streets:

Mathallen Oslo (Oslo Food Hall) - Mathallen is a thriving food market in Oslo that offers a diverse selection of local and foreign food goods, fresh vegetables, and specialized ingredients. It's an ideal location for sampling Norwegian cuisine and purchasing local delicacies.

District Grünerlkka (Oslo) - Grünerlkka is a popular neighborhood in Oslo recognized for its bohemian ambiance and quirky boutiques. Explore Thorvald Meyers gate and Markveien for independent boutiques, vintage stores, design shops, and one-of-a-kind fashion treasures.

Bergen Fish Market (Bergen) - The Fish Market is a busy and historic marketplace in the centre of Bergen where you can enjoy the bustling atmosphere and find an array of fresh fish, local goods, souvenirs, and traditional Norwegian crafts.

Bryggen (Bergen) - Bryggen is a UNESCO World Heritage site and renowned tourist destination in Bergen. This ancient dock district is adorned with beautiful wooden buildings and houses a variety of stores and boutiques selling traditional handicrafts, artwork, and clothes.

Bakklandet (Trondheim) - Bakklandet is a lovely Trondheim area notable for its small, cobblestone alleys and brightly colored wooden buildings.

Explore the neighborhood to find boutique boutiques, antique stores, cafes, and art galleries that showcase local workmanship.

Troms Market (Troms) - During the summer months, the Troms Market offers a wide variety of local products, including fresh seafood, fruits, vegetables, flowers, and handmade crafts. It's a fantastic place to learn about local culture and connect with sellers.

Stavanger Sentrum (Stavanger) - The city center of Stavanger is a lively neighborhood filled with stores, boutiques, and malls. Discover fashion retailers, design shops, and local boutiques on the pedestrian streets of vre Holmegate and Klubbgata.

Rros Marketplace (Rros) - Rros is a UNESCO World Heritage site known for its well-preserved wooden structures. The Rros marketplace provides a one-of-a-kind shopping experience with local foods, handicrafts, and traditional Norwegian souvenirs.

When visiting these marketplaces and retail streets, keep in mind that the hours of operation may differ. It's also worth exploring the neighboring areas since you can come upon hidden gems and smaller businesses selling locally manufactured products and crafts.

Practical Information

7.1 Emergency Phone Numbers and Contacts

Dial 112. For police, fire, or medical assistance in an emergency, dial 112.

Police: Dial 02800 for non-emergency police assistance.

Medical emergencies: Dial 113 if you need immediate medical attention.

Roadside assistance: Dial 987 if you are having automotive difficulty or require roadside assistance.

Dial 120 in the event of a marine emergency or an accident at sea.

Tourist Information: For particular questions regarding your region or attractions, contact local tourist information centers.

7.2 Health and Safety Advice for Visitors to Norway:

Medical Care: Healthcare in Norway is of high quality, and medical facilities are generally outstanding. European individuals can use the European Health Insurance Card (EHIC) to obtain necessary medical treatment. However, having travel insurance that covers medical expenses, including emergency evacuation, is still recommended.

Safety: Although Norway is regarded a safe country for travelers, it is always prudent to use common sense. Be mindful of your surroundings and take care to protect your personal goods, especially in crowded tourist locations.

Weather: The weather in Norway can be variable, especially in hilly locations. When engaging in outdoor activities, check weather forecasts and be prepared for changes in conditions.

Outdoor Safety: If you intend to participate in outdoor activities such as hiking or skiing, notify someone and check local weather and route conditions. Follow safety precautions, stay on designated paths, and bring the essential equipment, such as maps, adequate clothing, and enough food and water.

Road Safety: Although Norway's roads are well-maintained, driving conditions can be difficult in certain seasons, notably in winter. Learn the local traffic rules, pay attention to road signs, and modify your driving to the weather. Be prepared for limited services when driving in rural or remote places, and plan your fuel stops appropriately.

Outdoor Etiquette: Follow the "Leave No Trace" philosophy to respect nature and the environment. Leave the outdoors as you found it, dispose of rubbish correctly, and respect wildlife and protected areas.

Drinking Water: Norway's tap water is safe to drink and of high quality. Refilling your water bottle at taps and fountains across the country reduces the demand for single-use plastic bottles.

Before your journey, it is essential that you consult with official travel advisories and obtain up-to-date information to ensure you have the most accurate and relevant information regarding safety, health, and emergency contacts for your specific travel dates.

7.3 Norwegian Currency and Tipping Customs:

The Norwegian Krone (NOK) is the country's official currency. In hotels, restaurants, and shops, major credit cards are commonly accepted. ATMs are widely distributed across the country, and currency exchange services are provided at airports, banks, and exchange offices.

Tipping is not required in Norway because a service charge is frequently included in the bill. However, if you receive great service and want to express your gratitude, a tip of 5-10% is usually appreciated. In restaurants, it is customary to round up the bill or offer a tiny gratuity as a sign of appreciation. Taxi drivers appreciate modest gratuities as well.

7.4 Norwegian Customs and Etiquette:

Punctuality is highly valued in Norway, thus it is critical to arrive on time for appointments, meetings, and social occasions.
Personal Space: Norwegians place a high importance on personal space and privacy. When chatting with others, keep a reasonable distance and prevent unnecessary physical touch.

Queuing: Because Norwegians generally adhere to orderly queuing, it is vital to respect the queue and patiently wait your time.

Nature & Environment: Norway lays a great focus on environmental conservation. It is critical to respect nature, stick to marked pathways, and prevent littering. Be conscious of recycling activities and follow garbage disposal guidelines.

Dining Etiquette: Unless otherwise advised, it is traditional to remove your shoes upon entering someone's home. It is customary to wait for the host to begin eating before you begin, and utensils are commonly used when dining.

Drinking alcohol is allowed in Norway, however it is subject to laws. The legal drinking age for beer and wine is 18 and for spirits it is 20. Public intoxication is typically frowned upon, and driving while intoxicated is illegal.

Dress Code: In most settings, Norwegians dress casually. Smart-casual attire, on the other hand, may be appropriate for certain formal gatherings or upmarket eateries.

Social Equality: Norway values equality, and it is usual to treat everyone, regardless of social class or occupation, with respect and civility.

Following these etiquette and customs standards can help you navigate social situations in Norway while also showing respect for the local culture and traditions.

7.5 Communication and the Internet

Internet Access: Norway has great internet infrastructure, and internet coverage is widespread throughout the country. Customers may use free Wi-Fi in most hotels, restaurants, cafes, and public locations. Additionally, for internet access on your mobile devices, you can obtain a local SIM card or use roaming services from your mobile operator.

Mobile Networks: Several carriers, notably Telenor, Telia, and Ice, provide reliable mobile network coverage throughout Norway. Check with your mobile service provider about international roaming alternatives, or buy a local SIM card for lower local charges.

WhatsApp, Facebook Messenger, and Skype are popular communication programs that can be used for free texting and calls over Wi-Fi or mobile data.

7.6 Norway's Electricity and Plugs:

Norway's standard voltage is 230 volts, and the frequency is 50 hertz.

Norway employs the Europlug (Type C) and the Schuko (Type F) plug types. The Europlug has two round pins and two grounding clips on the sides, whereas the Schuko plug has two round pins and two grounding clips on the sides. If your devices have multiple plug types, bring a universal travel adaptor with you.

Before flying to Norway, verify the voltage and plug types of your electronic gadgets to ensure you have the necessary adapters or converters.

Norway's Sustainable Tourism

8.1 Norway's Responsible Travel Practices:

Norway is well-known for its dedication to environmental sustainability and responsible tourism. Here are some safe travel behaviors to consider when visiting Norway:

Nature and wildlife must be respected: Norway's natural beauty is its most valuable asset. Follow authorized pathways, avoid disturbing wildlife, and follow the "Leave No Trace" philosophy by not littering or disposing of waste appropriately. Respect protected places and adhere to any guidelines or limits that may be in place.

Support Local and Sustainable Businesses: Choose lodgings, restaurants, and tour operators who use environmentally friendly practices. Look for certificates that show environmentally beneficial practices, such as the Nordic Swan Ecolabel or the Green Key accreditation. Support local artisans, shops, and markets that sell handcrafted items.

Take Public Transportation: Norway has a well-developed and efficient public transportation system. When possible, use buses, trains, trams, and ferries instead of private vehicles. Public transportation minimizes carbon emissions and helps to lessen environmental impact.

Choose Eco-Friendly Activities: Choose eco-friendly activities that have a low environmental impact, such as hiking, biking, kayaking, or animal viewing. Choose tour providers that promote sustainability, such as those that offer low-impact whale watching trips or guided hikes with informed and experienced guides.

Conserve Energy and Resources: Be conscious of how much energy and resources you use. When not in use, turn off lights and electrical appliances, save water, and use resources wisely. To reduce single-use plastics, utilize reusable water bottles and bags.

Contribute to Conservation and Preservation Efforts: Consider donating to local conservation organizations or volunteering in environmental conservation projects. These efforts contribute to the preservation of Norway's natural environments and biodiversity.

Learn about Local Culture and Customs: When visiting new places, take the time to learn about the local culture, traditions, and customs. Local communities and their way of life must be respected. Before photographing someone, obtain their permission and be mindful of any cultural sensitivities or prohibitions.

By traveling responsibly, you can help to preserve Norway's natural and cultural heritage, reduce your environmental impact, and support the long-term development of local communities.

8.2 Nature Protection and Ecotourism in Norway:

Norway is well-known for its dedication to ecotourism and wildlife conservation. Here are some of the most important features of ecotourism and nature protection in Norway:

National Parks: Norway has many national parks that safeguard and preserve the country's unique ecosystems, such as mountains, fjords, forests, and wildlife habitats. These parks allow tourists to discover and appreciate the country's natural splendor while following sustainable principles.

Sustainable lodgings: To reduce their environmental impact, several Norwegian lodgings have embraced sustainable methods. Eco-lodges, wilderness cabins, and eco-friendly hotels are built using environmentally friendly materials, energy-efficient systems, waste management procedures, and resources supplied locally. Staying in such places contributes to sustainable tourism initiatives.

Wildlife Safaris: Visitors to Norway can go on wildlife safaris to see and learn about the country's native species, which includes whales, seals, seabirds, reindeer, and Arctic foxes. These safaris are led by knowledgeable guides that promote animal care and adhere to strict procedures to minimize disruption to the animals and their environments.

Sustainable Fishing and Hunting: Norway has rigorous legislation and procedures for sustainable fishing and hunting. Visitors can go on fishing expeditions or engage in appropriate hunting methods while being guided by qualified specialists who follow conservation rules and regulations.

Environmental Education and Interpretation: Environmental education and interpretation are important topics in many nature reserves, visitor centers, and guided tours in Norway. These programs seek to improve public awareness about the importance of nature protection, biodiversity, climate change, and environmentally friendly living habits.

Fjord Conservation: Norway's fjords are renowned natural features. Efforts are being done to safeguard and maintain the ecosystems of the fjords, which include water quality, marine life, and cultural legacy. To experience the fjords with reducing environmental effect, sustainable boating, kayaking, and cruise tours are available.

Norway is home to a number of research and conservation groups dedicated to the study and preservation of the country's unique natural settings. These organizations work on climate change projects, wildlife monitoring, habitat restoration, and conservation education.

Sustainable Transportation: Norway promotes the adoption of sustainable transportation solutions in order to reduce carbon emissions and the environmental impact of travel. Public transportation, electric vehicles, cycling, and walking are advocated as environmentally responsible alternatives to travel around the country.

Visitors who participate in ecotourism activities and support environmental conservation efforts in Norway help to maintain and preserve the country's natural legacy for future generations.

8.3 Norway's Sustainable Accommodation Options:

Norway has a variety of sustainable lodging options that prioritize environmental responsibility and environmentally sound techniques. Here are a couple such examples:

Eco-Lodges: Eco-lodges are accommodations that strive to reduce their environmental impact while providing comfortable facilities. These lodges frequently use renewable energy sources, waste management systems, and environmentally friendly building materials. They may also provide conservation and environmental awareness educational programs and activities.

Norway offers a network of wilderness cottages that are placed in scenic and secluded places. Organizations such as the Norwegian Trekking Association (DNT) often maintain and administer these cabins. They are intended to have a low environmental effect and to inspire people to connect with nature. Although the facilities are minimal, they provide a rare opportunity to responsibly experience Norway's wilderness.

Eco-Friendly Hotels: To lower their carbon footprint, many hotels in Norway have implemented sustainable practices. These hotels may use energy-efficient systems, renewable energy sources, recycling programs, and local community support via sourcing local products and services. Look for hotels that have received sustainability certifications such as the Nordic Swan Ecolabel or the Green Key.

Farm Stays: Farm stays allow you to experience rural life and reconnect with nature. These lodgings are frequently located on working farms that promote sustainable agricultural practices. Guests can learn about organic farming, eat locally sourced food, and relax in the countryside.

Green Camping: Norway has many camping areas that promote environmentally friendly camping methods. These locations may have recycling, waste management, and energy conservation facilities. They may also be located in environmentally vulnerable locations, where visitors are encouraged to respect and enjoy nature.

Wildlife Lodges: Wildlife lodges provide accommodations in certain areas that allow guests to responsibly observe and learn about local wildlife. These lodges are often created with a low environmental effect in mind, and they provide guided wildlife watching experiences that prioritize animal welfare and conservation.

Look for certificates or marks that reflect a dedication to sustainability when looking for sustainable hotel alternatives in Norway. Consider the hotel's efforts to save resources, reduce waste, assist local communities, and educate visitors about environmentally friendly practices. By choosing environmentally friendly hotels, you help to preserve Norway's natural and cultural heritage.

8.4 Norway's local and Community-Based Tourism:

In Norway, local and community-based tourism focuses on involving and helping local communities, protecting cultural heritage, and offering visitors with authentic and immersive experiences. Here are some features of Norwegian local and community-based tourism:

Cultural Immersion: Visitors to local and community-based tourism are encouraged to participate in local traditions, customs, and ways of life. It organizes cultural activities such as traditional festivals, music and dance performances, storytelling sessions, and handicraft workshops.

Homestays & Farm Stays: Staying with local families or on working farms allows visitors to experience authentic Norwegian hospitality while also learning about daily living. These lodgings offer a more intimate and authentic experience, frequently including home-cooked meals, shared activities, and opportunity to learn about local traditions and customs.

Local Guides and Tour Operators: Using local guides and tour operators guarantees that tourism benefits the community directly. These experts have extensive knowledge of the local geography, culture, and history, allowing guests to enjoy a more enriching and personalized experience. They may show you around lesser-known locations, tell you anecdotes, and give you a better insight of the local community.

Supporting local craftsmen and purchasing locally manufactured handicrafts, artworks, and products is an important part of community-based tourism. Look for chances to visit local craft workshops, cooperatives, and marketplaces where you may engage with artisans and buy one-of-a-kind, locally produced mementos.

Exploring local cuisine and dining at family-owned restaurants or cafés allows guests to appreciate traditional delicacies while also supporting local businesses. Consider participating in food tours, cooking workshops, or farm-to-table experiences that highlight regional delicacies and locally produced ingredients.

Community Initiatives and Events: To commemorate their heritage and engage visitors, many Norwegian communities arrange events, festivals, and cultural activities. These events allow visitors to mingle with residents, watch traditional performances, and take part in community activities. Examine local event calendars and inquire about community-based activities that will be taking place during your visit.

Responsible Nature Activities: Participating in nature-based activities with local guides and operators, such as guided walks, kayaking outings, or animal tours, ensures sustainable and respectful experiences. Environmental stewardship, wildlife protection, and reducing the impact on vulnerable ecosystems are frequently prioritized in these operations.

Local and community-based tourism contributes to the socioeconomic growth of local communities, the preservation of cultural traditions, and the promotion of mutual understanding and respect between visitors and residents. It enables a more real and meaningful travel experience while also benefiting the people and places you visit in Norway.

Visiting Norway with Children

9.1 Attractions for Families

When traveling with children in Norway, there are various family-friendly attractions that cater to children's interests and requirements. Here are some of Norway's best family-friendly attractions:

Museums and Interactive Centers: Norway has a number of museums and interactive centers geared at children. The Norwegian Museum of Science and Technology in Oslo, for example, provides hands-on exhibits, interactive displays, and workshops where children can learn about science and technology in a fun and engaging way. The Norwegian Folk Museum also has kid-friendly activities and exhibits that highlight Norwegian culture and history.

Amusement and Theme Parks: There are various amusement and theme parks in Norway that offer thrilling rides and entertainment for children of all ages. TusenFryd near Oslo is Norway's largest amusement park, including rides, roller coasters, and attractions ideal for both young children and teenagers. Kongeparken near Stavanger and

Hunderfossen Family Park in Lillehammer are also popular family attractions.

Outdoor activities: The natural landscapes of Norway offer several chances for outdoor activities ideal for children. Family-friendly treks and scenic walks are available at national parks, hiking trails, and nature reserves, where children may explore the outdoors, discover wildlife, and enjoy picnics in lovely settings. Popular family-friendly outdoor sites include Jotunheimen National Park, Rondane National Park, and Hardangervidda National Park.

Wildlife Safaris: Kids will love going on wildlife safaris to see the distinctive Norwegian fauna. Guided trips in places like Lofoten, Tromso, and Svalbard allow families to see wildlife like whales, seals, reindeer, and seabirds in their native habitats. The Polar Park in Bardu, northern Norway, is another interesting site where tourists can get up close and personal with wolves, bears, lynx, and other Arctic wildlife.

Norway offers various aquariums and wildlife parks where children may learn about marine life and interact with animals. The Bergen Aquarium is one of Norway's largest and most popular aquariums, where visitors may observe a variety of fish species, penguins, seals, and sea lions. The Polar Zoo in Bardu allows visitors to see Arctic species like as wolves, lynx, and musk oxen in their native habitat.

Train Rides and Boat cruises: Scenic train rides and boat cruises that showcase Norway's magnificent landscapes are popular among children. The Flam Railway in Flm is especially well-known for its spectacular journey through mountains, waterfalls, and fjords. Boat cruises around the fjords, such as the Geirangerfjord and the Naeryfjord, allow visitors to appreciate Norway's natural splendor from a new perspective.

Exploring historical monuments and cultural icons with children may be both informative and amusing. Fortresses, castles, and open-air museums such as Oslo's Akershus Fortress, Bergen's Bergenhus Fortress, and Oslo's Norsk Folkemuseum provide insights into Norwegian history, architecture, and traditional lifestyles.

These are just a few of Norway's many family-friendly attractions. The country is well-known for its child-friendly infrastructure, safe surroundings, and inviting culture, making it an ideal family vacation location.

9.2 Alternatives for Lodging

When traveling with children in Norway, it is critical to select accommodations that are appropriate for families and provide a comfortable and convenient stay. Consider the following lodging options:

Many Norwegian hotels include family-friendly services such as big family rooms, cribs or extra beds, children's play areas, and on-site restaurants with kid-friendly menus. Some hotels may also offer babysitting or leisure amenities such as swimming pools or game rooms. It is best to inquire ahead of time about the hotel's family-friendly amenities.

Renting an apartment or a vacation home can be a terrific alternative for families because it offers additional space and a more home-like environment. Apartments usually have separate bedrooms, a living area, and a fully equipped kitchen where you may cook meals and snacks for your children. This alternative provides flexibility and privacy, allowing you to choose your own schedule and routines.

Farm Stays: Farm stays are a tradition in Norway, where families may experience rural life while staying on working farms. These accommodations provide a one-of-a-kind experience for youngsters, allowing them to interact with animals, participate in farm activities, and learn about farming procedures. Farm stays frequently offer pleasant rooms or cottages as well as home-cooked meals made using locally sourced food.

Camping and Cabins: Norway is well-known for its scenic camping grounds and cabins nestled in the woods. Bathrooms, showers, and common kitchens are available on camping sites. Cabins with modest amenities such as mattresses, a small kitchenette, and heating are also available at some sites. Camping allows families to reconnect with nature and participate in outdoor activities such as hiking, fishing, and campfire evenings.

Hostels with Family Rooms: Many Norwegian hostels include individual family rooms or dorms intended exclusively for families. These rooms frequently include numerous beds or bunk beds, making them ideal for families with children.

Hostels are inexpensive options that can provide a social setting for families to meet other travelers.

Consider considerations such as location, access to attractions and amenities, safety, and reviews from other families when selecting lodging. It's also worth checking to see if the hotel offers amenities like laundry, high chairs, or baby equipment rental if necessary.

Remember to reserve your desired hotel well in advance, especially during high travel seasons.

9.3 Safety Recommendations and Guidelines

Keep Your Children Hydrated: Make sure your children drink enough of water, especially during outside activities and in hot weather. Carry water bottles and encourage frequent hydration breaks.

clothe Appropriately: Because the weather in Norway may be unpredictable, clothe your children in layers to accommodate shifting temperatures. For outdoor activities, bring rain gear, warm clothing, and comfortable shoes.

Sun Protection: Keep your children safe from the sun's rays by applying high-SPF sunscreen, wearing hats and sunglasses, and seeking cover during peak sun hours.

Road Safety: If you're traveling by automobile, make sure your children are properly restrained in car seats or booster seats. Follow traffic laws and drive carefully, especially on small and curving roads.

Water Safety: Always watch your children and make sure they are wearing life jackets when participating in water activities such as swimming or boating. Keep an eye out for any hazards and adhere to the safety rules offered by lifeguards or activity providers.

Wildlife Awareness: Norway is home to a variety of wildlife species, including moose and reindeer. Teach your children to keep a safe distance from wildlife and not to approach or feed it.

Stick to Marked Trails: When hiking or exploring nature trails, stay on marked tracks and heed safety warnings and instructions. Inform your children about potential dangers and risks, such as high cliffs and unstable ground.

Keep Up to current: Keep up to current on weather conditions, trail closures, and any safety cautions or warnings in the area you're visiting. Up-to-date information can be obtained through local tourist information centers, park authorities, or lodging providers.

Carry a list of emergency contact numbers, including local authorities, medical facilities, and the contact information for your lodging. Put emergency phone numbers on your phone for easy access.

9.4 Kids' Food and Dining Options in Norway:

Norway has a wide variety of cuisine and eating alternatives that can accommodate children's tastes and dietary preferences. Here are a few ideas:
Introduce your children to classic Norwegian cuisine such as fish cakes, meatballs, and potato dishes. The majority of restaurants and cafes serve child-friendly quantities or modified versions of popular local meals.

International Cuisine: Norway's larger cities have a diverse gastronomic scene that includes a number of international cuisines. Pizza, pasta, burgers, and sandwiches, which are normally popular with youngsters, are available.

eateries that openly emphasize family-friendly or child-friendly offerings: Look for eateries that explicitly promote family-friendly or child-friendly offerings. To keep youngsters entertained, these places frequently offer kid's menus, high chairs, and play spaces.

Self-Catering: If you want more control over your children's meals, try staying in a hotel with a kitchen. This allows you to cook dishes with locally sourced or familiar ingredients.

Snacks and Picnics: Keep nutritious snacks and portable foods on hand for your children to eat on the go. Fresh fruits, yogurt, sandwiches, and snacks appropriate for picnics or on-the-go meals are available in Norwegian stores.

Allergies & Dietary Restrictions: It is critical to explain your child's dietary restrictions or food allergies to restaurant personnel or caterers. Many businesses are accommodating and might offer other solutions.

It's also worth noting that tap water in Norway is safe to drink, so you can safely refill water bottles. Furthermore, supermarkets and convenience stores are readily available in most towns and cities, making it simple to obtain baby food, formula, or any other food products your child may want.

You may assure a safe and delightful gastronomic experience for the entire family in Norway by being attentive of safety and considering your children's dining tastes.

Culture and Language

10.1 Norwegian language Basics

Norwegian Language Fundamentals: Norwegian is the official language of Norway, specifically Standard Norwegian (Bokml). Here are some simple Norwegian phrases you could find useful during your visit:

: Hei
Goodbye: Ha det
Please: Vaer sa snill
Thank you very much: Takk
Yes: Ja
No: Nei
Please excuse me: Unnskyld Meg
Sorry: Beklager
Do you speak English?: Snakker du engelsk?
I don't understand: jeg forstar ikke

It's worth noting that many Norwegians, particularly in cities and tourist areas, speak English fluently. Communication in English is often extremely common and useful for travelers.

10.2 Cultural Practices and Customs:

The history, geography, and beliefs founded in egalitarianism, nature, and community all have an impact on Norwegian culture. When visiting Norway, keep the following cultural practices and customs in mind:

Punctuality is crucial to Norwegians, so appear on time for appointments, meetings, and social functions.

Personal Space: Norwegians are known to value personal space and privacy. Avoid unnecessary physical contact with others and respect their personal limits.

Norwegians have a strong connection to nature and enjoy outdoor activities. People are frequently seen hiking, skiing, and engaged in other outdoor activities. Respect the natural environment by adhering to leave-no-trace standards and following established trails.

Janteloven is a concept that stresses humility while downplaying individual accomplishments. Norwegians emphasize modesty and equality, thus they avoid boasting or unduly exhibiting money.

Tipping is not required in Norway because service charges are often included in the bill. However, as a token of appreciation for good service, it is customary to round up the amount or give a little tip.

Removing Shoes: It is traditional to remove your shoes while entering someone's home or certain institutions. If shoe removal is expected, look for signs or follow the host's lead.

Queuing: Norwegians commonly use a queueing system and respect those who wait in line. In public venues such as shops, sights, and transportation, be patient and wait your turn.

Nature Respect: Norwegians are environmentally concerned and prioritize sustainability. Trash should be disposed of responsibly, recycling requirements should be followed, and resources should be conserved.

Norway is well-known for its commitment to social equality. Respect and justice should be extended to everyone, regardless of gender, ethnicity, or social standing.

Alcohol Regulations: The sale and consumption of alcohol in Norway is strictly regulated. Alcoholic beverages having an alcohol concentration greater than 4.7% can only be purchased at Vinmonopolet outlets or licensed venues operated by the state.

You can have a more enriching and delightful stay to Norway if you respect Norwegian customs and cultural practices.

10.3 National Holidays and Traditional Festivities:

Norway has a number of national holidays and traditional festivities that are important to the country's culture and history. Here are some prominent Norwegian festivals and celebrations:

May 17th is Constitution Day. The most important national holiday in Norway, commemorating the signing of the Norwegian Constitution in 1814. It is celebrated throughout the country with parades, traditional costumes (bunads), music, speeches, and many cultural events.

Christmas (Jul): In Norway, Christmas is widely celebrated with traditions such as decorating Christmas trees, exchanging gifts, attending church services, and sharing festive feasts with family and friends. During the holiday season, many towns and cities have Christmas markets and concerts.

Easter (Pske): Easter is a significant festival in Norway, and it is celebrated with a variety of traditions such as egg decoration, skiing excursions, reading crime novels (an Easter tradition), and eating traditional Easter dishes such as lamb and marzipan.

Midsummer's Eve (Sankthansaften): Midsummer's Eve is a festival that welcomes the summer season and is celebrated on June 23rd. It involves outdoor gatherings, bonfires, music, dancing, and other folklore activities.

St. Olav's Day (July 29th): This holiday honors the death of St. Olav, Norway's patron saint. It is marked by religious processions, concerts, and cultural events, particularly in Trondheim, which is home to St. Olav's Cathedral.

Sami National Day (February 6th): Sami National Day celebrates and recognizes Norway's indigenous Sami culture. Traditional music, dance performances, cultural exhibitions, and events reflecting Sami traditions and customs are among the festivities.

10.4 Arts and Literature:

Norway is known for its rich artistic and literary legacy. The country has produced numerous well-known writers, poets, playwrights, and visual artists. The following are some noteworthy characteristics in Norwegian arts and literature:

Literature: Norwegian writers such as Henrik Ibsen, Knut Hamsun, and Sigrid Undset have achieved international acclaim. Contemporary authors such as Jo Nesb and Karl Ove Knausgrd have also made significant literary contributions.

Visual Arts: The visual arts in Norway cover a wide range of styles and mediums. The works of famous artists such as Edvard Munch and Nikolai Astrup have left an indelible mark on the art world. Norway also has a plethora of galleries and museums that exhibit both traditional and contemporary art.

Music: Norway has a thriving music culture that encompasses a wide range of genres and styles. Traditional Norwegian folk music, dubbed "Folkemusikk," incorporates instruments such as the

Hardanger violin. Norway is particularly well-known for its contributions to popular music, with singers such as A-ha, Kygo, and Sigrid reaching international acclaim.

Norwegian architecture combines modern ideas with a great respect for nature and sustainability. Snhetta's landmark works, such as the Oslo Opera House and the enlargement of Bergen International Airport, are examples.

Film: Norwegian filmmakers have received acclaim for their distinct storytelling and cinematic approach. The country has produced notable directors such as Joachim Trier and Bent Hamer, as well as films such as "Kon-Tiki" and "The Wave."

Visitors interested in discovering Norway's cultural legacy will find a broad and intriguing arts and literature scene. Museums, galleries, theaters, and cultural events allow you to become immersed in Norwegian artistic manifestations.

Additional Information

11.1 Useful Websites and Applications

Visit Norway (www.visitnorway.com): Norway's official tourism website gives detailed information on destinations, activities, lodging, transportation, and more.

Visit Oslo (www.visitoslo.com): The official tourism website for Oslo, providing thorough information on attractions, events, restaurants, and lodging in the capital city.

Visit Bergen (www.visitbergen.com): Bergen's official tourism website, with information on attractions, tours, events, and practical visitor suggestions.

Visit Troms (www.visittromso.no): Troms' official tourism website, with information on attractions, activities, events, and lodging in the Arctic city.

Visit Trondheim (www.visittrondheim.no): Trondheim's official tourism website, with information on sights, events, restaurants, and lodging in the city.

Norway Lights (www.norwaylights.com): An app and website that provides information about the Northern Lights in Norway, like as forecasts, viewing sites, and photography tips.

VisitNorway app: Visit Norway's official mobile app, which provides travel guides, maps, offline access, and tailored recommendations for seeing Norway.

11.2 Travel agents and tour Operators:

Fjord Tours (www.fjordtours.com): A prominent travel operator specializing in Norway trip packages such as fjord cruises, train journeys, and outdoor experiences.

Hurtigruten (www.hurtigruten.com): A cruise line that specializes on voyages around the Norwegian coast, offering one-of-a-kind opportunities to visit fjords, wildlife, and coastal communities.

Nordic Visitor (www.nordicvisitor.com): A travel service in Norway that specializes in personalized tours and self-drive itineraries, with a variety of options for visiting the country's highlights.

Outdoorlife Norway (www.outdoorlifenorway.com): A tour operator specializing in guided walks, fjord tours, and outdoor activities in Norway's breathtaking surroundings.

Up Norway (www.upnorway.com) is a luxury travel company that creates custom journeys and tailored experiences for discriminating tourists looking for unique and immersive encounters in Norway.

11.3 Embassies and Tourist Information Centers:

Tourist Information Centers: In major cities and towns throughout Norway, tourist information centers provide maps, brochures, and aid with travel planning. These centers are fantastic places to get up-to-date information on local attractions, activities, and events.

Embassies and Consulates: If you require consular help or have special questions about your country of residency, you can contact the Norwegian embassy or consulate. They can advise you on visa needs, safety precautions, and other pertinent travel information.

It is always best to check official websites and contact these resources directly for the most up-to-date and accurate information while planning a trip to Norway.